Heroes of Islām

By
Shaykh Mufti Saiful Islām

JKN Publications

First Published in September 2013

ISBN 978-1-909114-03-6

British Library Cataloguing in Publication Data
A catalogue record for this book is available from the British Library.

Publisher's Note:

Every care and attention has been put into the production of this book. If however, you find any errors they are our own, for which we seek Allāh's ﷻ forgiveness and reader's pardon.

Published by:

JKN Publications
118 Manningham Lane
Bradford
West Yorkshire
BD8 7JF
United Kingdom

t: +44 (0) 1274 308 456 I w: www.jkn.org.uk I e: info@jkn.org.uk

Book Title: Heroes of Islām

Author: Shaykh Mufti Saiful Islām

In the Name of Allāh, the Most Beneficent,
the Most Merciful

Contents

Introduction 6

The Holy Prophet ﷺ

Thinking of the Holy Prophet ﷺ.................................. 8

In the Hour of Triumph.. 10

Mercy of the Holy Prophet ﷺ................................... 12

Cheerful Manner of the Holy Prophet ﷺ.................... 14

Sayyidunā Umar ؓ

The River Nile... 17

Love and Hate for the Sake of Allāh ﷻ..................... 19

Sayyidunā Ali ؓ

Wise Sayings of Sayyidunā Ali ؓ............................... 21

Wisdom of Sayyidunā Ali ؓ...................................... 23

Sayyidunā Ali's ؓ intelligence.................................. 24

An Astonishing Verdict of Sayyidunā Ali ؓ................ 26

Companions of the Holy Prophet ﷺ 28

Sayyidunā Bilāl ؓ

A poem regarding Sayyidunā Bilāl's ؓ hardship in the path

of Allāh ﷻ... 30

Sayyidunā Salmān Al-Fārsi ؓ

An Inspiring Journey to Islām.................................. 31

Sayyidunā Hudhayfah Ibn Yamān ؓ

Love for Sunnah... 38

Sayyidunā Mus'ab Ibn Umayr ؓ

Sacrifice.. 41

Sayyidunā Salamah Ibn Akwa ؓ

The Brave Youth.. 43

Sayyidunā Saeed Ibn Āmir ﷺ

A Just Pious Ruler.. 46

Sayyidunā Abdullāh Ibn Abbās ﷺ

A Shining Example of Knowledge............................. 49

Sayyidunā Hasan and Husain ﷺ

Generosity.. 52

Sālim Ibn Abdullāh ﷺ

Only One Door... 54

Muhammad Ibn Qāsim ﷺ.. 55

Umar Ibn Abdul Aziz ﷺ

Caliph's Eid... 57

Zainul Ābideen ﷺ... 59

Thābit Ibn Nu'mān ﷺ... 62

Imām Abū Haneefah ﷺ

A Divine Foretelling... 64

Imām Sāhib's ﷺ Intelligence...................................... 65

Go and Perform Salāh for the Entire Night............. 66

A Wise Young Muslim Boy... 67

The Genius of Imām Abū Haneefah ﷺ..................... 70

A Neighbour in Need.. 71

Incidents of Intelligence.. 73

This is an Inspiration from Allāh ﷻ.......................... 79

The Distribution of the Deceased's Estate................ 79

The Tolerance of Imām Abū Haneefah ﷺ................. 80

The Genius of Imām Abū Haneefah ﷺ...................... 81

Stolen Goods are Recovered.. 83

Imām Abū Haneefah's ﷺ Answer is the Most Correct............. 84

The Understanding of Imām Abū Haneefah ﷺ............. 85

Wisdom of Imām Abū Haneefah 86

Selflessness and Sacrifice of Imām Abū Haneefah 87

Valuable Advice of Imām Abū Haneefah 90

Imām Mālik 94

Imām Shāfi'ee 97

Imām Ahmad Ibn Hanbal

His Birth & Life.. 101

Is there Such an Example?... 105

Imām Abū Yūsuf 108

The Justice of Qādhi Abū Yūsuf 110

The Fruits of Sincerity and Honesty............................... 111

Eight Lessons of Hātim Asamm 113

Sultān Salāh-ud-Deen Ayyūbi

The Power of Du'ā s... 117

Shareek Ibn Abdullāh

Justice is achieved.. 118

Noor-ud-Deen

The Ruler Standing Before a Judge............................... 122

Imām Wāqidi

Selflessness & Sympathy... 123

Ideal Ameer 125

Shams-ud-Deen Altamish

Allāh Granted me Four Qualities.................................... 126

A Very Special Dream... 128

Shaykh Qādhi Thanā-ullāh Pānipati 132

Shaykh Ashraf Ali Thānwi 134

Shaykhul-Islām Sayyid Husain Ahmad Madani 140

Shaykh Anwar Shāh Kashmiri 145

In the Company of Shaykh Mufti Tālib Uddin 150

In the Company of Shaykh Husain Ahmad Umarpuri ﷺ....... 155

Shaykh Muhammad Sarfarāz Khān Safdar ﷺ....................…..... 159

The Last Email of the Late Āsif Khalifah

An Eye-Opener for our Youth of Today............................... 165

Introduction

Praise be to Allāh ﷻ the Lord of the worlds and may peace and blessings be upon His final Messenger Muhammad ﷺ, upon his noble family, his Companions and upon those who follow their path until the final hour.

We live in a time and era where the success of a Muslim individual is dependent on the ink of the scholars. JKN Publications is proud to introduce this book "Heroes of Islām" exploring the lives of some of the greatest individuals in the history of Islām.

As humans we all need role models and who better to be our role models than the people who sacrificed their families, wealth and lives to honour this Deen. It is due to the sacrifices of such men that this Deen has come to us today and unless we follow their examples how will this Deen continue down to the generations to come.

This book is presented to our readers with the intention to create awareness of the lives and contributions of the great successors of our beloved Prophet Muhammad ﷺ.

One outstanding feature about this book is that it details the achievements of the Muslims in a historical order right from the early 6th century i.e. from the Holy Prophet Muhammad ﷺ to this current era. This can be divided into 6 categories:

1.   The life and achievements of our beloved Prophet ﷺ.
2.   The life and achievements of the Sahābah ؓ (Companions) of
      the Holy Prophet ﷺ.
3.   The life and achievements of the Tābi'een (successors of the
      noble Companions).
4.   The life and achievements of the Tabi-Tābi'een (successors of
      the successors of the noble Companions).
5.   The life and achievements of the A'imma-e-Mujtahideen (the
      four Imāms)
6.   Lastly the life and achievements of our pious predecessors.

I am delighted to be part of this exceptional book published by
JKN. It is another inspiring book prepared with great care for Muslims living in the western society.

I pray to Allāh ﷻ that He accepts this book and blesses my beloved
Shaykh, Mufti Saiful Islām abundantly for his efforts and valuable
time in preparing it.

I also pray that Allāh ﷻ makes this book a means of salvation for
my beloved Shaykh, for me and everyone else involved in its com-
pilation. Āmeen!

Maulanā Ibrāheem Khān
Graduate of JKN
September 2013

Thinking of the Holy Prophet 🕌

When becoming humiliated, remember the Holy Prophet 🕌 in Tāif.

When being starved, remember the Holy Prophet 🕌 tying two stones on his stomach in the Battle of the Trench.

When becoming angry, remember the Holy Prophet's 🕌 control of anger on the martyrdom of his beloved uncle Sayyidunā Hamzah 🕌.

When losing a tooth, remember the Holy Prophet's 🕌 tooth in the Battle of Uhud.

When bleeding from any part of the body, remember the Holy Prophet's 🕌 body covered with blood on his return from Tāif.

When feeling tired in Salāh remember the Holy Prophet's 🕌 blessed feet in Tahajjud.

When being pricked with thorns, remember the Holy Prophet's 🕌 pain from Abū Lahab's wife.

When being troubled by neighbours, remember the old woman who would empty rubbish on the Holy Prophet 🕌.

When losing a child, remember the Holy Prophet's 🕌 son Ibrāheem passing away.

When beginning a long journey, remember the Holy Prophet's ﷺ long journey to Madeenah without modern day transport.

When going against the Sunnah, remember the Holy Prophet's ﷺ intercession, "Ummati, Ummati, Ummati."

When sacrificing an animal remember the Holy Prophet's ﷺ sacrifice of 63 animals for his Ummah.

Before shaving your beard, remember the Holy Prophet's ﷺ face rejecting the two beardless Persians.

When falling into an argument with your wife, remember the Holy Prophet's ﷺ encounter with Sayyidah Ā'ishah﷽ and Sayyidah Haf-sah ﷽ .

When experiencing a shortage of food in the house, remember the Holy Prophet's ﷺ days of poverty.

When experiencing poverty, remember the Holy Prophet's ﷺ advice to As-hāb-e-Suffa (the people of Suffa).

When losing a family member, remember the Holy Prophet's ﷺ departure from this world.

When becoming an orphan, remember the Holy Prophet ﷺ at the age of six.

When sponsoring an orphan, think of the Holy Prophet's 珊 sponsor for Zaid Ibn Hārithah 錄.

When fearing an enemy, think of the Holy Prophet's 珊 saying to Sayyidunā Abū Bakr 錄 in Mount Thawr.
Whatever situation you may find yourself in, remember your role model, the best of creation; the Holy Prophet 珊.

In the Hour of Triumph

In the early stages of the Holy Prophet's 珊 life, the inhabitants of Makkah, with a few notable exceptions, persecuted him with non-stop and constant hatred. Not content with mere oppression, the Makkans at last hungered for his life and he migrated to Madee-nah.

After years of intense suffering, the Holy Prophet 珊 succeeded in winning the attention of a considerable body of his countrymen. They accepted his message and gathered under his flag to defend him and to defend their new Faith from the attacks of the pitiless enemies.

But the Makkans were still tireless in their hostility. In violation of the terms of the Treaty of Hudaibiyah, they attacked the clan of Banū-Khuzā'a that was under the protection of the Muslims and massacred a number of them. Banū-Khuzā'a appealed to the Holy Prophet 珊 for justice. The Holy Prophet 珊 at once marched with ten thousand warriors against the violators of peace and entered

Makkah practically unopposed.

Thus at last the Holy Prophet ﷺ entered the city he had been driven from, as a mighty conqueror. Those who had jeered at him as a dreamer, spat on his face, threw thorns in his path and laid the intestines of camels over his devoted head while prostrating in submission to Almighty Allāh ﷻ, were there before him - now defeated and broken.

Those who had imprisoned him and tried to starve him to death, those who had surrounded his house in the darkness of night with murderous intention and those who exiled him from his dear native land, they were all there and at his complete mercy. Those who had attacked him again and again, wounded his forehead with stones, broke his teeth and killed his nearest relatives and comrades before his eyes they were there that day, weak and helpless. Those who had ruthlessly hunted him even in his exile, those who had disgraced humanity by inflicting shameless cruelty upon innocent men and women and even upon the dead body of his companions, they too were there humbled at his feet.

But there was no sign of anger or hatred in the face of the Holy Prophet ﷺ. On the contrary, his feature blossomed up in mercy to men and gratitude to Allāh ﷻ. In the hour of triumph every evil suffered was forgotten, every injury inflicted was forgiven and a general forgiveness was proclaimed to the population of Makkah. The army emulated his example. No house was entered into, no inhabitant molested, no woman insulted.

Then the Holy Prophet ﷺ addressed the gathering and declared in his own unique voice, "All glory and victory belong to Allāh ﷻ and to Allāh ﷻ alone. No one has any superiority over his neighbour except for his virtue. All are children of Ādam ﷺ. The noblest of men is he who is foremost in good deeds."

The Holy Prophet ﷺ paused for a moment and looked at his enemies still trembling in their hearts. No one could say if any poisoned memory of the bygone days flashed across his mind at their sight. But he addressed them in a calm voice, "Descendants of Quraish, how do you expect I should treat you?" They replied, "With kindness and pity, gracious brother and nephew."

Tears filled the eyes of the Holy Prophet ﷺ at these words and he said, "I shall speak to you just as Sayyidunā Yūsuf ﷺ spoke to his brothers. I shall not reproach you today. Allāh ﷻ will forgive you. He is the most Merciful and Compassionate."

Mercy of the Holy Prophet ﷺ

Sayyidunā Abū Hurairah ﷺ narrated a story of a man from Banū Haneefah named Thumāmah Ibn Uthāl who was taken prisoner by the Muslims.

After the Muslims captured him, this leader of Yamāmah was tied to a pillar in the Masjid. The Holy Prophet ﷺ came out to him and said, "What is with you, O Thumāmah?"

He replied, "O Muhammad, I have much with me that is good, and if you kill me then you are killing one that has many relatives. If you show favour to me, then you are showing favour to one that is thankful. If you wish for wealth, then ask and you shall be given wealth."

The Holy Prophet ﷺ left him, then returned the next day and asked him again, "What is with you, O Thumāmah?" He replied, "It is as I have told you."

The Holy Prophet ﷺ left him only to return the following day and asked him again, "What is with you, O Thumāmah?"

He said, "With me is what I have said to you. If you show kindness, then you are showing kindness to one that is thankful. If you kill, you are killing one who has a large clan, and if it is wealth that you desire, I can provide you with wealth."

The Holy Prophet ﷺ said to his Companions, "Free Thumāmah."

Thumāmah went to a date-palm tree near the Masjid, washed himself, entered the Masjid and declared: "I bear witness that no one has the right to be worshiped but Allāh ﷻ and I bear witness that Muhammad is His Messenger and servant."

He said, "O Muhammad, by Allāh ﷻ, there was no face that was more hatred to me than your face and now it has become the most beloved face to me. By Allāh ﷻ, there was no religion that was more hatred to me than your religion and now it is the most beloved to me. By Allāh 鐄, there was no land that was more hatred to me than your land and now your land has become the most beloved to me...I wish to perform Umrah..."

The Holy Prophet 鐄 upon hearing this wish, gave him glad tidings and told him to act upon his noble intention. When he went to Makkah, someone said to him, "Indeed you have rebelled." He replied, "No, indeed I have accepted Islām with the Holy Prophet 鐄, and by Allāh 鐄, you will not receive even a grain of wheat from Yamāmah, unless the Messenger of Allāh 鐄 allows it."

Cheerful Manner of the The Holy Prophet 鐄

Our beloved Prophet 鐄 was a jovial and jolly person. He would sometimes joke with people, but always within limits and with affection.

Once a blind man was in the presence of the Holy Prophet 鐄 and asked, "O' Messenger of Allāh 鐄! will I be able to also enter Jannah?" The Holy Prophet 鐄 replied, "No my dear brother, no blind person will enter Jannah."

The blind person started to cry. The Holy Prophet 鐄 smiled and said, "Brother, no blind person will ever enter Jannah in the state of blindness; rather he will be given sight." Upon hearing this the man became pleased.

Once an elderly lady Sahābi came to the Holy Prophet ﷺ and requested that he make Du'ā for her entry into Jannah. The Holy Prophet ﷺ said, "No old lady will enter Jannah." She began to cry, whereupon the Holy Prophet ﷺ said, smiling, "An old lady will not enter into Jannah, rather she will be made young and then entered into Jannah." Upon hearing this she became happy.

Once the nursing mother of the Holy Prophet ﷺ, Sayyidah Umme Ayman ﷺ came to the Holy Prophet ﷺ and requested a camel from him. The Holy Prophet ﷺ told her, "I will give you a child of a camel." She sadly said, "What will I do with a child of a camel?"

The Holy Prophet ﷺ then indicated to a servant of his, who brought a young camel and presented it to Sayyidah Umme Ayman ﷺ. The Holy Prophet ﷺ smiled and told her, "Is this not also a child of a camel? All camels are the children of other camels." Upon hearing this she smiled.

A Sahābiyyah (female companion) once came in the presence of the Holy Prophet ﷺ and requested, "O' Rasūlullāh ﷺ! My husband is ill, make Du'ā for his recovery." The Holy Prophet ﷺ told her, "Is it your husband whose eyes have whiteness?" She was puzzled and immediately went home and opened her husband's eyes. He asked her, "What's the matter?" She replied, "Rasūlullāh ﷺ told me that my husband's eyes have whiteness in them." He started smiling and said, "Is there any person whose eyes have no whiteness in them?" Only then did she understand the humorous remark of the Holy Prophet ﷺ. The intention of the Holy Prophet ﷺ was to bring some happiness to her husband.

Our beloved Prophet ﷺ was soft natured and had a pleasant character. He never hurt the feelings of anyone and always spoke in affectionate terms to others. The tolerance of the Holy Prophet ﷺ was always friendly and warm. His tongue was so sweet that everyone benefited from him.

A person came to the door of the Holy Prophet ﷺ and requested permission to enter. The Holy Prophet ﷺ replied, "Let him enter, even though this person is not a good person from amongst his tribesmen." When he entered, the Holy Prophet ﷺ greeted him warmly and spoke gently to him. When he left, Sayyidah Ā'ishah asked in great surprise, "O' Rasūlullāh ﷺ! In your esteemed opinion this person is not a good person, and yet you spoke and dealt with him very cordially and kindly?" The Holy Prophet ﷺ replied, "In the sight of Allāh ﷻ, the worst person is he who people avoid because of his crude manner and evil tongue."

Once when a drought fell on Madeenah, a person by the name of Ubbād Ibn Sharjeel, out of hunger, went into an orchard, picked some fruit from a tree, ate some and kept some aside. The owner of the orchard caught him, beat him and took off his clothes. Ubbād complained to the Holy Prophet ﷺ. The owner of the orchard was also present. He explained the theft of Ubbād.

The Holy Prophet ⚜ said, "He is a naive person, you should have treated him with affection and warmth. He was hungry, you should have fed him."

The Holy Prophet ⚜ then had Ubbād's clothes returned to him and also gave him a quantity of grain.

Sayyidunā Umar ⚜
The River Nile

After Egypt was conquered by the Muslims, the newly appointed Governor of Egypt, Sayyidunā Amr Ibnul Ās ⚜ one day held an open discussion in his court. Someone told him, "O Leader! During the ancient times, there was a custom which the locals practiced that kept the River Nile flowing. On the 11th day of every lunar month, we would take a young girl, with the consent of her parents, adorn her with the best of clothes and finest jewellery and sacrifice her to the River Nile."

When he heard this, Sayyidunā Amr Ibnul Ās ⚜ objected that this practice is most certainly not acceptable or permissible in Islām. Islām has come to remove such barbaric and evil customs. That year, this custom was abandoned and it so happened the River Nile started drying out. Many people were forced to abandon their homes and migrate.

Sayyidunā Amr Ibnul Ās ⚜ narrated this entire episode by letter to the Ameerul Mu'mineen, Sayyidunā Umar ⚜.

17

Sayyidunā Umar ⚊ wrote back that indeed Islām has come to destroy such evil customs. Together with the reply, he wrote another letter, which he said should be thrown into the River Nile.

The Governor read out this letter, which contained the following, "From the servant of Allāh ﷻ Umar, Ameerul Mu'mineen to the River Nile. If you flow on your own accord, then do not flow, but if Allāh ﷻ, The One and Mighty, makes you flow, then we beseech Allāh ﷻ, The One and Mighty to make you flow."

The governor of Egypt threw this letter into the River Nile and the next morning when the people awoke they saw that during the course of one night, Allāh ﷻ had made the River Nile rise by more than 100 hand-lengths. In this way, Sayyidunā Umar ⚊ put an end to the evil custom of girl sacrifice. The greatness of Allāh ﷻ also manifested that ever since that time the River Nile has continued flowing.

It is indeed true that whosever becomes Allāh's ﷻ, Allāh ﷻ becomes his. When Allāh ﷻ becomes his then all the creation of Allāh ﷻ obeys his instructions.

The Sahābah ⚊ had sacrificed everything of theirs for Allāh ﷻ. Hence, Allāh ﷻ had made the entire creation subservient to them. We should endeavour to follow the footsteps of the Sahābah ⚊ in our daily lives.

Love and Hate for the Sake of Allāh ﷻ

Sayyidunā Umar ؓ once entered the Masjid and noticed that a pipe from Sayyidunā Abbās's ؓ gutter was located in the property of the Masjid, because of which the water from his roof would flow into the Masjid property. Sayyidunā Umar ؓ reasoned that since this pipe was benefiting a single person only, it was against the respect of the Masjid to have it there. He therefore gave the instruction for the pipe to be removed. Although he never gave the instruction out of anger, he gave it because his anger was for Allāh ﷻ.

When Sayyidunā Abbās ؓ found out about this, he approached Sayyidunā Umar ؓ and asked why the pipe was taken down. Sayyidunā Umar ؓ explained to him that the Masjid was not a private property and therefore not permissible for any person to use the property for his own benefit.

"Do you know how that pipe came to be there?" Sayyidunā Abbās ؓ asked. "It was there at the time of the Holy Prophet ﷺ and the Holy Prophet ﷺ himself gave permission for it to be placed there. Who are you to have it removed?"

"Did the Holy Prophet ﷺ really give permission for it to be there?" Sayyidunā Umar ؓ asked. "He certainly did," Sayyidunā Abbās ؓ replied. "Come with me then," Sayyidunā Umar ؓ said to

19

Sayyidunā Abbās ⸙. They then went to the place where the pipe was and Sayyidunā Umar ⸙ bent down in the bowing position. "Now get on my back and replace the pipe," Sayyidunā Umar ⸙ said. "I will rather get someone else to do it," said Sayyidunā Abbās ⸙.

However Sayyidunā Umar ⸙ insisted, "How was I to take down something that the Holy Prophet ﷺ allowed to be put up? Because I have committed such a serious wrong, the least punishment I can suffer is for you to stand on my back and replace the pipe." Sayyidunā Abbās ⸙ then did as Sayyidunā Umar ⸙ had instructed and the pipe has remained where it was till today.

May Allāh ﷻ reward those who have built the Masjid leaving the pipe where it had been even though it had no use. They have done this as a reminder and the practice upon the Hadeeth of the Holy Prophet ﷺ.

The Holy Prophet ﷺ said, "Whoever loves for the sake of Allāh ﷻ and dislikes for the sake of Allāh ﷻ has perfected his Imān."

Sayyidunā Ali ﷺ
Wise Sayings of Sayyidunā Ali ﷺ

- The punishment of involving yourself in the love of material aspects is the deprivation of true love for Allāh ﷻ.
- Miserliness is the clothing of dishonour.
- Do not be satisfied with the results of that person whose heart is not in his work.
- It is easier to turn a mountain into dust, than to create love in the heart that is filled with hatred.
- The person who follows his desires will surely get lost.
- Bravery is that you exercise patience for a little while.
- Moderation is the best status in all affairs.
- Your best friend is that person who assists you the most in time of your needs.
- It is better to refrain from sins than to seek forgiveness later.
- The person who is ensnared by jealousy will be ensnared by a 'bad' ending.
- Many diseases and problems are due to extravagance.
- An intelligent enemy is sometimes better than a foolish friend.
- Ability to do something is good fortune and helplessness is misfortune.
- The person who points out and looks for faults in others, opens the door of exposing his faults to others.
- The person who assists a brother at times of difficulty, Allāh ﷻ will assist him in his time of need.
- The person who is saved from the tongue of others is fortu-

nate.

- The person who saves himself from vulgar language will find success.
- Every act that is beneficial is Sadaqah (charity).
- Many strange people are better than your own relatives.
- Many of the drowned are those who have been sunk in the sea of ignorance.
- Many are the learned whom the world has destroyed.
- The best of your wealth is that which is of most benefit to you in times of need.
- Whoever loves this world, he is in reality accumulating his wealth for others.
- During the day man's actions are always changing, so appreciate those days in which you are able to do good actions.
- At the time of reaching the extremes of difficulty and hardship, then know that the time of ease has to come.
- The man who is living in ease cannot appreciate the level of difficulties of others.
- The person who has very little wealth and means of happiness will only have ease and comfort at death.
- Sometimes a little increases and becomes a lot and sometimes a great deal decreases to nothing.
- To ask brings dishonour and to give creates love.
- A little, well earned which satisfies your needs will suffice you better than a lot which is spent extravagantly.
- The greater the degree of happiness, so much at the end of it will be your difficulty, loss or grief.

- The company of bad or evil people causes a good person to also be regarded as evil.
- Some are great people but people do not value them.
- A respected person always remains honourable even if he is afflicted with difficulties.
- He will not be lost who keeps on asking the way.
- A person will not be perplexed who makes Mashwara (consultation) with others.
- A cautious and intelligent person is he who does not rely on his own opinion and judgement.
- A person who is satisfied with his own actions will have many that dislike him.
- The person whose self is precious in his own eyes then his desires will be valueless to him.
- The person who regards minor difficulties as major, Allāh ⚬ will afflict him with major difficulties and problems.

Wisdom of Sayyidunā Ali ⚬

The following episode illustrates the wisdom and ingenuity of Sayyidunā Ali ⚬.

Two companions along a journey sat down to eat. One companion had five bread rolls and the other had three. A passer by, on the invitation of the two companions, joined them. After eating, the generous passer-by presented them with eight Dirhams (silver coins).

The traveller who had three bread rolls requested his companion to share the money equally between them. The companion refused, saying that he was entitled to five Dirhams since he had five bread rolls. The other one should receive three Dirhams because he had three rolls. When they could not settle the dispute, they presented their case to Sayyidunā Ali ﷺ who said to the one who had three bread rolls, "What harm is there if you accept this division of three and five?" He replied, "I want justice." Sayyidunā Ali said, "If it is justice you want, then you take one Dirham and your companion seven Dirhams."

The companion with three bread rolls objected. Sayyidunā Ali ﷺ commented, "There were eight rolls and three who ate, hence each person ate one third of the eight rolls. Eight consists of 24 thirds. Thus each one ate eight parts. However, his three rolls consists of 9 parts. After having consumed his 8 parts there remained one part of his share. The one with five rolls had 15 parts of which he ate 8, leaving behind 7 parts. The 8 Dirhams have therefore to be divided in this proportion, the one who contributed one part of his bread has to receive one Dirham and the one who contributed 7 parts should receive 7 Dirhams."

Sayyidunā Ali's ﷺ Intelligence

Two men left a substantial amount of money in the custody of a Quraishi lady. When leaving their Amānat (trust), they instructed her to return it to them only when both call together. Under no circumstances was she to hand over the Amānat to only one of them.

After a year, one of them appeared claiming that his partner had died. He demanded the return of the money. The lady refused and reminded him of the condition the two had fixed for the return of the Amānat. The man was stubborn in his demand. He refused to leave. He caused a big disturbance in the neighbourhood, complaining loudly. The residents forced the lady to return the money. Ultimately she relented.

After some time the second man appeared and requested the Amānat. The lady was confused. She explained what had transpired, but he refused to accept her explanation, saying that she was guilty of violating the agreement. He demanded that she compensates him since she was at fault.

The dispute was brought to Sayyidunā Ali ﷜. After he heard both parties, he concluded that the two had tricked the lady. He said to the man, "Did the two of you not stipulate that she should hand over the Amānat only when both come?" The man readily agreed. Sayyidunā Ali ﷜ said, "Your money is by me. Bring your friend and collect it." The device of the fraud was thus unsuccessful.

An Astonishing Verdict of Sayyidunā Ali ﷺ

Rasūlullāh ﷺ had dispatched Sayyidunā Ali ﷺ to Yemen. The people of Yemen had a tradition of digging a ditch in order to trap a lion. Once a lion was made to fall into a ditch through various tactics, they would then hunt it. They once trapped a lion in one such ditch. The people gathered around this ditch in such great numbers that it became virtually uncontrollable for those who were on the brink to keep balanced. One person ultimately lost his balance and was about to fall in the ditch, upon this he held the hand of one of the adjacent men (who were watching) and he too lost his balance. This second man in turn held the hand of a third man and the third the hand of a fourth man. Eventually all four fell into the ditch. The lion was still alive and was furious and hence mauled all four of them. They all succumbed to their injuries and died immediately.

A row then erupted amongst the deceased people's kith and kin as to who was responsible for the deaths and who was going to give Diyyat (blood money or compensation for manslaughter). The row grew more aggressive and swords came out from all sides. Blood was about to be spilt! In such a traumatic and delicate circumstance it was Sayyidunā Ali ﷺ who intervened and after calming down the situation gave his verdict.

The primary responsibility of these deaths lay with the digger of the ditch and he would be made to pay Diyyat (blood money). They would be compensated in such a manner that the first person got a quarter of the blood money, the second person got one third of the blood money, the third person got half of the blood money and the last got the full amount. When the matter went to the Holy Prophet ﷺ he approved of it.

Imām Qurtubi ﷫ explains this astonishing verdict of Sayyidunā Ali ﷜ in the following words: "All four of the deceased lost their lives through manslaughter and the ditch digger was responsible for it. However the first person being a victim of the manslaughter was also a murderer of the other three persons by pulling their hands while falling into the ditch. His blood money would be divided into four equal parts and he would get only one and the victims get one part each. Similarly, the second person was the murderer of two persons and his blood money would be divided into three equal parts and he got only one part of it. The third person was the murderer of just one person so his blood money would be divided into two and hence he gets half of it. The last one was not responsible for any further deaths so he would get the whole of the blood money." (Tafseer-e-Qurtubi)

Companions of the Holy Prophet
A Poem Regarding the Sacrifice of the Companions

The Sahābah ﷺ are those who the Holy Prophet ﷺ saw or they saw him, and they took the Shahādah and died as a Muslim.

For the Deen of Islām, each one of them surely did sacrifice, and this is why Allāh ﷻ gave them the certificate of Paradise.

They were a group of people the likes of which you won't now find, and they led their lives in a way that's an example for the whole of mankind.

They gave their health, wealth and time to spread Islām, but they also gave the same to defend the Deen and make sure it came to no harm.

Their level of Imān would reach such highs, that Jannah and Jahannam would come in front of their eyes.

Look at the lives of Abū Bakr, Umar, Uthmān and Ali ﷺ, who were the Khulafā-e-Rāshideen, to follow in their footsteps, we should all be ready and keen.

In the Battle of Uhud, Hamzah, Mus'ab and Hanzalah ﷺ, all became Shaheed, so to have their valour and courage, is something we all need.

Khadeejah, Āishah, Fātimah or Sumayyah, women should try to be like them, or any of the Sahābiyyah.

Hasan, Husain, Usāmah, Salmān and Zaid ؓ, if the youngsters copy them, then their future Inshā-Allāh will be made.

Abū Hurairah, Abū Dardā, Ibn Umar, Ibn Abbās and Ibn Mas'ood ؓ, we need to have hunger for Deeni knowledge like them, 'cos' it's our spiritual food.

Bilāl, Khabbāb, Abū Zar, Yāsir and Ammār ؓ, if we undergo their sacrifice in life, we'll go very far.

Khālid, Sa'd and Ja'far ؓ, were all brave and heroic Mujāhids, so they have to be role models for us and our kids.

But to try and be like any of the Sahābah, should be our aim and measure, because they are the ones who are guaranteed Allāh's ﷻ pleasure.

Be it the Mujāhir of Makkah or the Ansār of Madeenah, if we aim to be like them, then Inshā-Allāh we'll be on the road to Jannah.

Just like the bright star in the dark sky, is the example of the Sahā-bah, whoever follows any of them in this world, will reach their destination in Ākhirah.

Sayyidunā Bilāl ☙

A Poem Regarding Sayyidunā Bilāl's ☙ Hardship in the Path of Allāh ﷻ

Sayyidunā Bilāl ☙ was an Ethiopian slave, who accepted Islām, because it was Allāh's ﷻ pleasure which he did crave.

But because he became a Muslim, he went through a lot of suffering and pain, because his owners would beat him and tie him with a chain.

In beating him the disbelievers would take it in turn, and then they'd lie him in the scorching heat for him to burn.

They'd place a rock on him, as he lay on the burning sand, but he wouldn't renounce Islām, which was the disbelievers demand.

The people would see Sayyidunā Bilāl's ☙ state and think he was mad, because all he would say was "Ahad! Ahad! Ahad!"

He wouldn't be affected by the torture or the burning heat, because his Imān was so strong and it was Allāh ﷻ that he wanted to please and meet.

The disbelievers would see Sayyidunā Bilāl's ☙ suffering and start laughing, but they soon shut up when Sayyidunā Bilāl ☙ had the honour of being the Holy Prophet's ﷺ Muaddhin.

Once in his dream, the Prophet ﷺ was in Jannah, and he heard Sayyidunā Bilāl's ؓ footsteps before him, so look how Allāh ﷻ elevated Sayyidunā Bilāl ؓ, and made him an example for every single Muslim.

He was a slave who wasn't even an Arab, but he became a very eminent famous Sahābi. So when we as Muslims go through any suffering, pain or strife, we should take lessons by looking at Sayyidunā Bilāl's ؓ life.

Sayyidunā Salmān Al-Fārsi ؓ
An Inspiring Journey to Islām

This is a story of a 'Seeker of Truth', set in the days of the past. It is of a man who once lived in Persia. To begin with, from his own words:

I grew up in the town of Isfahān in Persia in the village of Jayyan. My father was the Dihqān or chief of the village. He was the richest person there and had the biggest house in his area.
Since I was a child, my father loved me, more than he loved any others. As time went by, his love for me became so strong and overpowering that he feared to lose me or have anything happen to me. So he kept me at home, a real prisoner, in the same way that young girls were kept.

I became devoted to the Magian religion so much so that I attained the position of custodian of the fire which we worshipped. My

31

duty was to see that the flames of the fire remained burning and that it did not go out for a single hour, day or night.

My father had a vast estate which yielded an abundant supply of crops. He himself looked after the estate and the harvest. One day he was very busy with his duties as chief of the village and he said to me, "My son, as you see, I am too busy to go out to the estate now. Go and look after matters for me today."

On my way to the estate, I passed a Christian church and the voices of prayer attracted my attention. I did not know anything about Christianity or about the followers of any other religion throughout the time my father kept me in the house away from people. When I heard the voices of the Christians I entered the church to see what they were doing. I was impressed by their manner of praying and felt drawn to their religion. "By God," I said, "This is better than ours. I shall not leave them until the sun sets."

I asked and was told that the Christian religion originated in Ash-Shām (Greater Syria). I did not go to my father's estate that day and at night I returned home. My father met me and asked what I had done. I told him about my meeting with the Christians and how I was impressed by their religion. He was dismayed and said, "My son, there is nothing good in that religion. Your religion and the religion of your forefathers is better." "No, their religion is better than ours." I insisted.

My father became upset and afraid that I would leave our religion. So he kept me locked up in the house and put a chain on my feet. I managed however to send a message to the Christians asking them to inform me of any caravan going to Syria. Before long they got in touch with me and told me that a caravan was heading for Syria. I managed to unfetter myself and in disguise accompanied the caravan to Syria. There, I asked who was the leading person in the Christian religion and was directed to the Bishop of the church. I went up to him and said, "I want to become a Christian and would like to attach myself to your service, learn from you and pray with you."

The bishop agreed and I entered the church in his service. I soon found out, however, that the man was corrupt. He would order his followers to give money in charity while holding out the promise of blessings to them. When they gave anything to spend in the way of God, however, he would hoard it for himself and not give anything to the needy and poor. In this way he amassed a vast quantity of gold. When the bishop died and the Christians gathered to bury him, I told them of his corrupt practices and at their request, showed them where he kept their donations. When they saw the large jars filled with gold and silver they said, "By God, we shall not bury him." They nailed him on a cross and threw stones at him. I continued in the service of the person who replaced him. The new bishop was ascetic who longed for the Hereafter and engaged in worship day and night. I was greatly devoted to him and spent a long time in his company.

After his death, this man 'the seeker of truth' attached himself to various Christian religious figures, in Mosul, Nisibis and elsewhere. The last one had told him about the appearance of a man of God in the land of the Arabs who had a reputation of strict honesty, one who would accept a gift but would never consume charity for himself. The man 'the seeker of truth' continues his story.

A group of Arab leaders from the Kalb tribe passed through Ammuriyah and I asked them to take me with them to the land of the Arabs in return for whatever money I had. They agreed and I paid them. When we reached Wādi Al-Qurā (the place between Madeenah and Syria), they broke their agreement and sold me to a Jew. I worked as a servant for him and eventually he sold me to a nephew of his, belonging to the tribe of Banū Qurayzah. This nephew took me with him to Yathrib, the city of Palm trees.

At that time the 'Man of God' was inviting his people in Makkah to Islām, but I did not hear anything about him then because of the harsh duties which slavery imposed upon me.

When the 'Man of God' reached Yathrib, I was in fact at the top of a palm tree belonging to my master doing some work. My master was sitting under the tree. A nephew of his came up and said, "May God declare war on the Aws and Khazraj (the two main Arab tribes of Yathrib). By God they are now gathering at Qubā to meet a man."

I felt hot flushes as soon as I heard these words and I began to shiver so violently that I was afraid that I might fall on top of my master. I quickly got down from the tree and spoke to my master's nephew, "What did you say, repeat those words to me." My master was very angry and gave me a terrible blow. "What does this matter to you? Go back to what you were doing," he shouted.

That evening I took some dates that I had gathered and went to the place where the 'Man of God' had arrived. I went up to him and said, "I have heard that you are a righteous man and you have companions with you who are strangers and are in need. Here is something from me as Sadaqah (charity). I see that you are more deserving for it than others." The 'Man of God' ordered his companions to eat but he himself did not eat from it. I gathered some dates and when the 'Man of God' left Qubā for Madeenah, I went to him and said, "I noticed that you did not eat from the charity I gave. This however is a gift for you." Of this gift of dates, both he and his companions ate.

The strict honesty of the 'Man of God' was one of the characteristics that led the man (the seeker of truth) to believe in his teachings and accept Islām. The 'Man of God' was none other than the final Messenger of Allāh, Muhammad ﷺ. The man 'seeker of truth' is the illustrious companion of the Holy Prophet ﷺ, Sayyidunā Salmān Al-Fārsi ﷺ.

Sayyidunā Salmān Al-Fārsi ﷺ was released from slavery by the Holy Prophet ﷺ who paid his Jewish slave owner a stipulated price and who himself planted an agreed number of date palms to secure his freedom. After accepting Islām, Sayyidunā Salmān

Al-Fārsi ﷺ would say when asked whose son he was, "I am Salmān, the son of Islām from the children of Ādam."

Sayyidunā Salmān Al-Fārsi ﷺ was to play an important role in the struggles of the growing Muslim state. At the Battle of the Trench, he proved to be an innovatory military strategist. He suggested digging a ditch or Khandaq around Madeenah to keep the Quraysh army at bay. When Abū Sufyān (not yet a Muslim), the leader of the Makkans, saw the ditch, he said, "This strategy has not been employed by the Arabs before."

Sayyidunā Salmān Al-Fārsi ﷺ became known as "Salmān the Good". He was a scholar who lived a rough and ascetic life. He had one cloak which he wore and on which he slept. He would not seek the shelter of a roof but stayed under a tree or against a wall. A man once said to him, "Shall I not build you a house in which to live?" "I have no need for a house," he replied. The man persisted and said, "I know the type of house that would suit you." "Describe it to me," said Sayyidunā Salmān Al-Fārsi ﷺ. "I shall build you a house which if you stand up in it, its roof will hurt your head and if you stretch your legs the wall will hurt them."

Later, as a governor of Al-Madā'in near Baghdād, Sayyidunā Salmān Al-Fārsi ﷺ received a salary of five thousand Dirhams. This he would distribute as Sadaqah. He lived from the work of his own hands. When some people came to Mada'in and saw him working in the palm groves, they said, "You are the leader here and your sustenance is guaranteed yet you do this work!" "I like to eat from the work of my own hands," he replied. Sayyidunā Salmān Al-Fārsi ﷺ however was not extreme in his asceticism.

It is related that he once visited Sayyidunā Abū Dardā ﷺ with whom the Holy Prophet ﷺ had joined in brotherhood. He found Sayyidunā Abū Dardā's ﷺ wife in a miserable state and he asked, "What is the matter with you?" "Your brother has no need of anything in this world," she replied. When Sayyidunā Abū Dardā ﷺ came, he welcomed Sayyidunā Salmān Al-Fārsi ﷺ and gave him food. Sayyidunā Salmān Al-Fārsi ﷺ told him to eat but Sayyidunā Abū Dardā ﷺ said, "I am fasting." "I swear to you that I shall not eat until you eat also," said Sayyidunā Salmān Al-Fārsi ﷺ. Sayyidunā Salmān Al-Fārsi ﷺ spent the night there as well. During the night, Sayyidunā Abū Dardā ﷺ got up but Sayyidunā Salmān Al-Fārsi ﷺ got hold of him and said, "O Abū Dardā, your Lord has a right over you, your family has a right over you, give to each its due." In the morning, they prayed together and then went out to meet the Holy Prophet ﷺ. The Holy Prophet ﷺ supported Sayyidunā Salmān Al-Fārsi ﷺ in what he had said.

Sayyidunā Salmān Al-Fārsi ﷺ might easily have been a major figure in the sprawling Persain Empire of his time because of the influential household in which he grew up. His search for truth however led him, even before the Holy Prophet ﷺ had appeared, to renounce a comfortable and affluent life and even to suffer the humiliation of slavery. According to the most reliable account, he died in the year 35 Hijri.

Sayyidunā Hudhayfah Ibn Yamān ﷺ
Love for Sunnah

Sayyidunā Hudhayfah Ibn Yamān ﷺ was a Sahābi who gave his life for the Holy Prophet ﷺ and was also one to whom the Holy Prophet ﷺ told his secrets. He was therefore famously known as the Holy Prophet's ﷺ secret carrier.

Persia was a superpower at the time and their way of life was famous all over the world. Although the Romans were also a superpower during those times, the people of Persia were famously known for their cleanliness.

It was at the time when the Muslim army was about to attack the Persian army that the Persians invited the Muslims to talks. Amongst the people that went for the talks was Sayyidunā Hudhayfah ﷺ. When they arrived, the Persians had some food prepared for them to eat, so the Muslims sat down to eat. As they were eating, a morsel of food slipped from Sayyidunā Hudhay-fah's ﷺ hand and fell down.

The teaching of the Holy Prophet ﷺ is that when this happens, a person should pick up the food, clean it, recite Bismillāh and eat it because it is not known in which morsel the blessings of the food is found. As he bent down to pick it up, another person knocked his elbow to ask him what he was doing because he was not to do that in the presence of the Persians who would think that it was a dirty thing to do.

The person felt that the Persians would think that the Muslims are ill mannered people who do not know how to eat or people who do not have such good food, because of which they wish to pick it up. He was therefore telling Sayyidunā Hudhayfah 🙵 to leave the food for once.

Now listen to the unique reply that Sayyidunā Hudhayfah 🙵 gave him. He said, "Should I leave out the Sunnah of Rasūlullāh 🙵 for the sake of these fools?"

He did not care what the Persians thought about his action, whether they would laugh, mock or feel bad about it. He could not leave out the Sunnah of the Holy Prophet 🙵 and therefore picked up the morsel, cleaned it, recited Bismillāh and ate it.

We must also teach these examples to others and always practice on the Sunnah no matter how embarrassing it may seem.

When Sayyidunā Hudhayfah 🙵 and Sayyidunā Rib'ee Ibn Āmir 🙵 went to attend the talks with the Persians and were entering the palace, Sayyidunā Rib'ee 🙵 was still wearing his old clothing, which may also have been untidy after a long journey.

When he reached the gates of the palace, the doormen stopped him saying, "You cannot go and see our king looking like that!" They gave Sayyidunā Rib'ee 🙵 a long garment to wear. To this Sayyidunā Rib'ee 🙵 said, "If I have to wear that to see your king, then I would rather not go and if I have to go, then I will go in my own clothing. If he does not wish to see me in these clothes, then I do not wish to see him either. I shall then rather go back."

The doorman then sent a message saying that strange people have arrived who do not want to wear our clothing to enter. As he waited, Sayyidunā Rib'ee ﷺ started to mend the strips of cloth that covered the broken parts of his sword. Looking at the sword, the doorman said, "May I have a look at that sword?" When Sayyidunā Rib'ee ﷺ handed it over to him, the doorman laughed, "Are you going to conquer Persia with that?" Sayyidunā Rib'ee ﷺ said, "You have only seen the sword but have not seen the arm that uses the sword."

"Then show me your arm," the doorman said. "If you want to see my arm," Sayyidunā Rib'ee ﷺ said, "You must fetch the strongest shield you have." The doorman then brought an iron shield that they knew could never be damaged by a sword. "Now bring someone to hold it," Sayyidunā Rib'ee ﷺ said. When one of the soldiers held the shield, Sayyidunā Rib'ee ﷺ struck it so forcefully with his sword that the shield broke into two pieces. The soldiers watching were stunned and sent a message inside the palace that such strange people have come who break shields in half with their swords.

It was the custom of the Persians that the king usually sat on a throne while everyone else stood. However, when Sayyidunā Rib'ee ﷺ arrived he said, "We do what our beloved Prophet ﷺ taught us and amongst his teachings were that one person cannot be sitting while others stood and spoke. Either you have chairs for us all as well or you stand like the rest of us." This made the king furious and he gave the command that Sayyidunā Rib'ee ﷺ be sent away with a pot of sand on his head. Sayyidunā Rib'ee ﷺ took the sand and put it on his head. As he left, he said to the king, "You have already given us the sand of your territory."

The Persians were very superstitious people and every little statement worried them. They therefore thought it is a terrible thing that they had given their land away to the Muslims. The king therefore sent someone to get the pot back. How could he get it back from someone like Sayyidunā Rib'ee ﷺ! Sayyidunā Rib'ee ﷺ got away with the sand because Allāh ﷻ had already decided that the Muslims should free the land of the Persians.

Sayyidunā Mus'ab Ibn Umayr ﷺ
Sacrifice

Sayyidunā Mus'ab Ibn Umair ﷺ was brought up with great love and affection by his wealthy parents. Before becoming a Muslim, he lived in luxury and comfort. It is said that he was the most well dressed youth in Makkah. In fact, his parents would buy him outfits worth two hundred Dirhams. He became a Muslim in the early days of Islām, without his parents knowing. When they came to know of it, they tied him with a rope and compelled him to stay at home. He got an opportunity to escape and migrated to Ethiopia.

On return from Ethiopia, he migrated again to Madeenah. So a person like him, brought up in luxury and comfort, was now living a simple and hard life. The Holy Prophet was once sitting with the Sahābah when Sayyidunā Mus'ab passed in front of him. He had only one sheet of garment to clothe his body and this also had many patches. One of the patches was of leather. With tears in his eyes, the Holy Prophet spoke about Sayyidunā Mus'ab's life of luxury before Islām.

In the battle of Uhud, Sayyidunā Mus'ab held the flag of Islām. When the Muslims started to suffer defeat and were running about in confusion, he held the flag and stood at his post like a rock. An enemy came out and cut his hand with a sword, so that the flag may fall and the defeat may be accomplished. He at once took the flag in the other hand. The enemy then cut the other hand also. He held the flag to his chest with the help of his bleeding arms. The enemy at last pierced his body with an arrow. Only then did he fall to his death and with him the flag also fell which he had not allowed to fall while he was alive. Another Muslim ran and took the flag.

At the time of his burial, he had only one sheet to cover his body. This sheet was too short for his size. When it was pulled to cover the head, the feet would be exposed, and when it was pulled to cover his feet, the head would become uncovered. The Holy Prophet said, "Cover his head with the sheet and his feet with grass."

Such was the end of the youngster who was brought up in luxury and comfort. The person who used to wear clothing worth two hundred Dirhams does not have sufficient cloth to cover his dead body! Look with what courage he tried to keep the flag up and did not allow it to fall till he was martyred. This is the miracle of Imān. Once Imān enters a person, it makes him forget everything else, whether it is wealth, luxury or life itself.

May Allāh ﷻ grant us the ability to follow in the footsteps of the Sahābah ⬩ and may Allāh ﷻ enlighten their graves with Noor. Āmeen!

Sayyidunā Salamah Ibn Akwa ⬩
The Brave Youth

Sayyidunā Salamah Ibn Akwa ⬩ was a Sahābi of the Holy Prophet ﷺ. He was very active and alert, he was also an expert archer. One day an interesting event occurred. On the outskirts of Madeenah there was a jungle called Ghāba, where the camels of the Holy Prophet ﷺ grazed. Some robbers attacked and killed the shepherd and stole the camels. All this occurred in the last portion of the night just before true dawn. Sayyidunā Salamah Ibn Akwa ⬩ took his bow and arrows and set off for the jungle before Fajr Salāh, when someone informed him of this event.

Sayyidunā Salamah ⬩ immediately ascended a mountain and faced towards Madeenah proclaiming, "Dacoits (robbers) have attacked! Come quick to the rescue!"

43

Upon making this announcement, Sayyidunā Salamah ؓ set off in pursuit of the robbers on his own. He reached them quickly and shot off a valley of arrows, reciting the following, "I am Ibn Akwa, and today is the day when you will remember your nursing days!"

The aim of Sayyidunā Salamah ؓ was flawless, achieving success at every strike, either wounding or killing his targets. At first the robbers were under the impression that they were being attacked by a group of Muslims, and they bolted with terror. It was only sometime later that they realised they were being followed by only one youth.

The robbers tried to capture him but as anyone of them turned around, Sayyidunā Salamah ؓ would hide behind a rock or tree and strike at the horse of his pursuer, thereby wounding it. The robbers would then flee in terror.

Sayyidunā Salamah ؓ relentlessly pursued them. They were so frightened that they left the camels of the Holy Prophet ﷺ behind and ran to save their lives. They even abandoned their excess luggage and weapons. They abandoned 30 cloaks and 30 spears.
The robbers sought the assistance of another group of robbers. They were now prepared to attack Sayyidunā Salamah ؓ. Sayyidunā Salamah ؓ climbed a mountain and called out, "I am Ibn Akwa! I take an oath on that Being Who has granted the honour to Muhammad ﷺ that none of you will be able to catch me, and I can get any one of you I desire!"

The robbers were struck with terror and they halted. Sayyidunā Salamah ⚬ stalled them by talking, awaiting some assistance from Madeenah. Within a short time he noticed a group of horsemen of Sahābah ⚬ who were coming to his assistance.

As they reached an opening, a battled ensued. After a while the leader of the robbers was killed and the rest of them fled. Sayyidunā Salamah ⚬ once again chased them. He remained at their heels until the evening. The robbers stopped at the oasis to drink some water. When they saw Sayyidunā Salamah ⚬ gaining on them they fled in fear and terror without having taken any water.

One of their men lagged behind. Sayyidunā Salamah ⚬ ran behind him and released an arrow, proclaiming, "I am Ibn Akwa! Today is the day of destruction for the evil!" The arrow struck the man's shoulder who cried out in pain, "Are you the same Ibn Akwa of this morning?"

Thereafter, Sayyidunā Salamah ⚬ seized two horses of the robbers and presented himself before the Holy Prophet ⚬ where he noted that the Sahābah ⚬ had gathered the cloaks and spears abandoned by the robbers and the camels of the Holy Prophet ⚬. Sayyidunā Bilāl ⚬ slaughtered one of the camels and was roasting its liver and hump for the Holy Prophet ⚬.

Sayyidunā Salamah ⚬ requested the Holy Prophet ⚬, "Depute 100 men with me and we will pursue the robbers and finish them off!"

The Holy Prophet ﷺ taking note of his youth and vigour smiled and said, "There is no need for further chasing. Those people must have reached their tribe by now!"

They rested for the night, and when they set off the next morning towards Madeenah, the Holy Prophet ﷺ granted Sayyidunā Salamah ؓ the honour of sitting with him on his camel.

Sayyidunā Saeed Ibn Āmir ﷺ
A Just Pious Ruler

It has been related that Sayyidunā Umar ؓ appointed Saeed Ibn Āmir ؓ as the governor of Hims. When Sayyidunā Umar ؓ visited the region, he said, "O people of Hims! How do you find your governor?" They complained to him, saying that they had four complaints about him, "He does not come out to us until late in the morning." Sayyidunā Umar ؓ said, "That is grave indeed! And what else?" "He does not answer anyone during the night." Sayyidunā Umar ؓ said, "Grave indeed! And what else?" "One day during every month, he does not come out to us!" Sayyidunā Umar ؓ said, "Grave indeed! And what else?" "Every so often, he is in a miserable and wretched state."

Sayyidunā Umar ؓ gathered both Saeed Ibn Āmir ؓ and those who complained about him, in order to issue judgement regarding those accusations, which if proven to be true, would prove him to be an unfit governor.

When Sayyidunā Umar gathered everyone, he said, "What is your complaint regarding him, O people of Hims?" They said, "He does not come out to us until late in the morning." Sayyidunā Umar said, "And what do you say, O Saeed?" Saeed said, "By Allāh, O Leader of the Believers! Although I hate to mention it, my family has no servant. So, I am responsible for making the bread (from the early stages of the process to the end), and then I make ablution, after which I go out to the people."

Sayyidunā Umar said, "And what else do you complain about regarding him, O people of Hims?" They said, "He does not answer anyone during the night." Sayyidunā Umar said, "And what do you say, O Saeed?" He said, "Although I hate to mention it, O Leader of the Believers! I have indeed made the day for them and the night for Allāh."

"And what else do you complain about regarding him, O people of Hims?" They said, "One day during every month, he does not come out to us!" "And what do you say O Saeed?" He said, "O Leader of the Believers! I have no servant who may wash my garment, and I have no other garment to replace it, so I wash it until it dries and then I go out to them at the end of the day."

Sayyidunā Umar then asked, "And what else do you complain about him, O people of Hims?" They said, "Every so often, he is in a miserable and wretched state." "And what do you say, O Saeed?" He said, "I witnessed the death of Khubayb Al-Ansāri in Makkah, the Quraish cut parts of his flesh into pieces. They then

47

carried him to the root of a tree and crucified him. They said. 'Do you wish that Muhammad was in your place, and that you were with your family and with your children?' He said, 'By Allāh ⬡, I do not wish that I was with my family and my children nor that Muhammad ⬡ was pricked by a thorn!' Whenever I remember that day and how I did not help him in the state that he was in. I was a disbeliever at the time and did not believe in Allāh ⬡, the Almighty. I start to think that Allāh ⬡ will never forgive me for that sin, and then I enter into a state of extreme misery."

Sayyidunā Umar ⬡ said, "All praise is to Allāh ⬡, Who has not made me fail in my observance." He then sent for 1,000 Dinars to be given to Saeed ⬡ and he said, "Use this to help you in your affair!"

Saeed's ⬡ wife said, "All praise is for Allāh ⬡, Who has given us enough so that we do not need your (i.e. Saeed's ⬡ work in the house) services anymore." He said, "Do you wish for better than that? We give it to someone who will bring it to us when we are most in need of it."

She said, "Yes." He called someone from his household that he trusted in, and he put the money in a bag, saying, "Go with this money to the widow of such and such man, with this amount to the orphan of such and such parents, with this money to such and such poor person, and with this money to such and such person who is afflicted." Very little was left with him, and he said to his family, "Spend from this!" He returned to his work, and his wife said to him one day, "Will you not buy a servant for us! What happened to that wealth?" He answered her, saying, "It will come to you when you are in need of it most!"

Sayyidunā Abdullāh Ibn Abbās ⌖
A Shining Example of Knowledge

This great Sahābi ⌖ earned the following Du'ās from the Holy Prophet ⌖ because of the service, honour and respect he showed for him, "O' Allāh ⌖! Bless him with the understanding of Deen and the interpretation of the Kitāb." (Bukhāri)

Sayyidunā Abdullāh Ibn Abbās ⌖ had made great strides and efforts in acquiring Deeni knowledge. He had also attained a high level of humility and modesty. It never occurred to him that he should be given preference because he was the cousin of the Holy Prophet ⌖ and a close family member.

Had he counted on the fact that he was a close relative of the Holy Prophet ⌖, then he would have never attained such high ranks purely because of this honour.

In his quest for knowledge he had undergone such great difficulties and toiled so much, that such effort is unheard of in our times, amongst our students. His condition was such that whenever he required anything from anyone, he would not call that person to him, but would go to the person himself. If he realised that the person was resting, then he would wrap himself up in his shawl and wait on that person's doorstep, ignoring the dust and sand which settled on his body.

When the person emerged from his home, he would enquire from him what he needed to know. This person would tell him that he is the cousin of the Holy Prophet 🙽, and he should not have undergone such difficulty. He would tell Sayyidunā Abdullāh Ibn Abbās 🙽 that he should have summoned him instead. Sayyidunā Abdullāh Ibn Abbās 🙽 would say that he is the one seeking knowledge; hence he needed to present himself, regardless of difficulty.

Sometimes he would wait for a long time, but he never had the notion that the person should abandon his own duties and come to him. The fruits of all his effort earned him expertise in the fields of Tafseer, Hadeeth, Fiqh, poetry, speech and many other fields of knowledge.

Despite his young age, he acquired the status of being one of the senior Sahābah of the Holy Prophet 🙽. Sayyidunā Umar 🙽 would place him amongst the senior Sahābah 🙽 from whom he would take advice.

Sayyidunā Umar 🙽 was asked as to why he would consult Sayyidunā Abdullāh Ibn Abbās 🙽 inspite of the presence of many senior Sahābah 🙽. He replied, "He is well-spoken, intelligent and an intellectual young boy."

Abū Saleem 🙽 asked Tāwoos 🙽 why he only referred to this young boy, in the presence of many of the senior Sahābah ﷺ? He replied, "I have seen that many Sahābah ﷺ of the Holy Prophet ﷺ, when they discuss any Mas'alah, they would refer to him." Allāh ﷻ has also gifted him such that whenever he spoke, he did so in such a sweet way, where the listener became engrossed.

He always had a crowd of people surrounding him. He had also given his entire life to the imparting of Deeni knowledge. At times there would be so many students outside his home, that a passer-by would find it difficult. He would satisfy the thirst of everyone seeking knowledge with ease and contentment, and none would leave disappointed.

When knowledge and practice enters one's heart, then that heart becomes illuminated and shines brightly. Such fear of Allāh ﷻ overwhelms that heart that everything else pales into insignificance.

Sayyidunā Abdullāh Ibn Abbās ﷺ was the cousin of the Holy Prophet ﷺ, and also from the side of the Holy Prophet's ﷺ wife, Sayyidah Maymūnah ﷺ the Holy Prophet ﷺ was his maternal uncle (the Holy Prophet ﷺ was the husband of his mother's sister).

(Seeratus-Sahābah)

He remained in the service of the Holy Prophet ﷺ during his childhood, where he displayed a great degree of love and affection. He never remained behind in inviting people towards Islām. Even though he had attained a high rank and status, his eyes were always wet with the tears shed in fear of Allāh ﷻ.

Having spent his entire life from childhood to old age in the service of Deen, this great servant of Islām was finally laid to rest in the year 68 AH. He had reaped the rewards of sacrifice for Islām and the Holy Prophet ﷺ. Through constant fear of Allāh ﷻ he had attained a high level of Taqwā and purity. When he was finally laid to rest in his grave a voice from the unseen called out, **"O contented soul! Return to your Lord, pleased with Him & He pleased with you." (89:27-30)**

Sayyidunā Hasan and Husain ﷺ
Generosity

Abul Hasan Madāini ﷺ relates that once, Sayyidunā Hasan ﷺ, Sayyidunā Husain ﷺ and Sayyidunā Abdullāh Ibn Ja'far ﷺ were going for Hajj. The camels carrying their provisions were lost on the way and they continued their journey without food or drink. They came upon a Bedouin tent, in which there sat an old woman, and on asking her, if she had anything to drink, she said that she had. So they dismounted from their camels. The old woman had only one she-goat, which was very thin and lean. She asked them to milk it and share the milk among themselves. They did so and drank its milk dividing it among themselves. Then they asked the old woman if she had anything to eat and she said, "I have got this she-goat only, but if you slaughter it, I shall cook its meat for you."

They slaughtered the goat, which the woman cooked and served to

them. They ate to their fill and in the evening when they were going to start their journey, they said to her, "We are Hāshimites and
we are going for Hajj; when after Hajj, we get back to Madeenah
safe and sound, do visit us there, we shall repay you for your hospitality, Inshā-Allāh." After they had departed, the old woman's
husband came back home from the forest, and she told him all
about the guests from the Banū Hāshim.

He was angry and scolded at her saying, you slaughtered your
goat for strangers; you don't know who they were and where they
came from. How do we know they were Hāshimites?" He was silent after rebuking her.

In the course of time, the old man and his wife became very poor
and went to Madeenah to look for some odd jobs to earn their living. During the day, they used to gather dried camel dung (which
was used as fuel), which they sold in the evening, thus earning
themselves a bare living.

One day the old woman was gathering some camel dung as usual
when she passed in front of the house of Sayyidunā Hasan ﷺ who
saw her and, recognising her, sent his servant to invite her to come
into his house. When she came, Sayyidunā Hasan ﷺ said to her,
"Do you know me?" When she said that she didn't, he replied, "I
am your guest who drank the milk of your she-goat and then
slaughtered it to eat its meat." The old woman still did not
recognise him and said, "My Lord! Are you the same person ?" He
again told her that he was the same guest and ordered his men to

buy a thousand goats for her, which were immediately purchased
and gifted to the old lady, together with a thousand Dinārs (gold
coins) in cash. Sayyidunā Hasan ؓ then sent her, in company with
his servants, to his younger brother, Sayyidunā Husain ؓ who
asked her how much his elder brother had given her in return for
her hospitality and, when he was told about it, he also gave her a
thousand goats and a thousand Dinārs in cash.

Sayyidunā Husain ؓ sent her, in turn, to Sayyidunā Abdullāh Ibn
Ja'far ؓ who, when he learnt what the two brothers had gifted her,
gave her two thousand goats and two thousand Dinārs in cash,
saying, "If you had come to me before going to Sayyidunā Hasan
ؓ, I would have given you even more money in reward." The old
woman went to her husband with four thousand goats and four
thousand Dinārs and said to him, "Here is something in return for
our thin and weak goat." (Ihyā ul Uloom)

Sālim Ibn Abdullāh ﷺ
Only One Door

Sālim ﷺ was the grandson of Sayyidunā Umar Fārooq ؓ. He was
near the Ka'bah one day when he met Hishām Ibn Abdul Malik,
who was the king of the time. Hishām greeted Sālim ﷺ and said,
"Please tell me if there is anything that you need and I will see that
it is done." Sālim ﷺ said, "O' Hishām! I feel ashamed to ask from
anyone else when I am right in front of Allāh's ﷻ house. Our respect for Allāh ﷻ does not allow us to stretch our hands before
anyone else but Allāh ﷻ." Hishām could say nothing and kept si-

lent.

It so happened that Sālim ﷺ left the Haram at the same time that Hishām did. When Hishām saw Sālim ﷺ outside, he came close and asked, "You may now tell me how I can be of service to you." However, Sālim ﷺ said, "Tell me what it is I can ask from you? Can I ask for Deen or for something of this world?"
Hishām knew well that as far as Deen was concerned, Sālim ﷺ was one of the greatest scholars of the time. He therefore said, "You may ask me for something of this world." Sālim ﷺ immediately said, "I have never asked for anything of this world even from Allāh ﷻ. How can I then ask it from you?!"

Hishām was shocked to learn that there really are people who ask all their needs only from Allāh ﷻ. The truth is that people who know how to ask from Allāh ﷻ will never stretch their hands out before people.

Muhammad Ibn Qāsim ﷺ

Muhammad Ibn Qāsim ﷺ was born in the city of Tāif. His father was Qāsim Ibn Yūsuf who passed away when Muhammad Ibn Qāsim ﷺ was very young, leaving his mother in care of his education. His paternal uncle, Hajjāj Ibn Yūsuf Ath-Thaqafi, an Umayyad Governor, was very instrumental in teaching Muhammad Ibn Qāsim ﷺ about warfare and governance. He married his cousin Zubaidah, Hajjāj's daughter, shortly before going to Sindh (in modern day India). His conquest of Sindh and Punjab laid the foundations of Islamic rule in the Indian subcontinent.

When Muhammad Ibn Qāsim 靐 attacked and conquered Sindh he was only seventeen years old and a General for the Umayyad Caliphate. Usually children at that age cannot even run a house properly, let alone an army! He was however the commander of the Muslim army that came to defeat the powerful army of Rājah Dāhir.

The armies of Muhammad Ibn Qāsim 靐 and Rājah Dāhir met on a vast battlefield and after a hard fight, the army of Muhammad Ibn Qāsim 靐 defeated the enemy on the strength of their Imān.

It is written in the books of history that when some thieves from Rājah Dāhir's men looted a caravan of Muslim women, one of the women called out, "Help us!" "Help us!" Muhammad Ibn Qāsim 靐 said, "I am at your service, my sister!" It was therefore in reply to this call that Muhammad Ibn Qāsim 靐 led the Muslim army against Rājah Dāhir. After defeating Rājah Dāhir, Muhammad Ibn Qāsim 靐 did not stop but marched forward up to Multān to make sure that Islām reached there as well.

Umar Ibn Abdul Aziz ﷺ
Caliph's Eid

Four eminent successors of the Holy Prophet ﷺ are well known to the world. After them Umar Ibn Abdul Aziz ﷺ was a very prominent Caliph.

Historian's Estimate

The historians call him 'Umar the Second'. Some historians are of the opinion that he should be ranked among the Khulafā-e-Rāshideen in view of his personal virtues and attributes, zeal for propagating the cause of religion and enthusiastic efforts towards the establishment of an Islamic order.

When he became Caliph, Muslim power was at its zenith. On the occasion of an Eid which fell during his reign, the well-to-do Muslims demonstrated a spirit of joy. All the people, rich and the poor, got costly garments prepared and indulged in ostentation and show. On seeing this, the sons of Ameerul-Mu'mineen Umar Ibn Abdul Aziz ﷺ, followed suit. They appeared before their mother and said, "Dear mother! Tomorrow will be Eid. All the people are getting new dresses prepared for their children. We have not a single cloth which is free from patches. Please get some new clothes for us. It is not proper for us to celebrate Eid in these ragged clothes."

The mother tried all night to discourage them, but in vain. Their obstinacy grew beyond measure. The mother of the children,

Fātimah, went to the Caliph. The Caliph sat on a prayer mat wearing worn out clothes. He was absorbed in prayers in a most submissive manner with tears in his eyes and his beard wet.

Fātimah, the Caliph's wife was much impressed by this scene. In a very sympathetic tone she said, "Ameerul-Mu'mineen! It is Eid today. All the people are rejoicing while you are weeping on this occasion." The Caliph replied, "Full month of Ramadhān has passed. What a blessed month it was! What a good opportunity for righteousness and piety was given to us. I am not sure if we have derived enough benefit from this golden opportunity to correct ourselves. Have we gathered as much virtues as could be sufficient to save us from the accountability before Allāh 🌟? I think I have missed the whole Ramadhān." As soon as he uttered these words he became unconscious. Although he was the Ameerul-Mu'mineen he had neither perfume nor rose-water in his house. Water was sprinkled over him to bring him to his senses, he enquired of his wife, Fātimah, as to why she had come to him.

Fātimah replied, "The children did not let me sleep throughout the night. They have been insisting on having new clothes for Eid. Their argument is that as they are the sons of Ameerul-Mu'mineen, it is not right for them to celebrate Eid in old clothes while the people in general will be celebrating Eid in glittering costumes. This has compelled me to approach you and put my request to you."

The Caliph said, "You too, pretend to be ignorant. Where is the money to make them garments with? As you are well aware, I get only two Dirhams daily from state treasury, which can hardly suffice our daily needs. How can I afford to arrange for new clothes?"

Fātimah replied, "You are Ameerul-Mu'mineen, after all the treasury is in your hands. You may take money out of it." The Caliph said, "What is in the treasury is not mine but belongs to all the Muslims. I am nothing but a trustee. I cannot take any thing without their permission. Do you desire that I am blamed for the charge of mistrust for fulfilling the desire of my sons and make myself liable to the punishment of the Hereafter?"

Zainul Ābideen 🌸

Zainul Ābideen 🌸 said, "Some people worship Allāh 🌸 because of fear. This is the Ibādah of slaves. Some worship Him because of their desire for Thawāb, this is the Ibādah of the traders. Some worship Him in gratitude for His bounties. This is the Ibādah of freed slaves."

Charity in Concealment

Many poor and destitute people were obtaining their needs without being aware of their benefactor. Zainul Ābideen 🌸 exercised great care to conceal his acts of charity. He arranged for his charitable contributions to be delivered to the poor during the night.

He concealed his charity so much that some people being unaware of his generosity branded him a miser. Only when he died was it discovered that a hundred families were secretly supported by him. These families too were not aware who their benefactor was, while Zainul Ābideen ﷺ was alive.

Refrain from the Friendship of 4 People

Bāqir ﷺ narrates, "My father (Zainul Ābideen ﷺ) instructed me not to associate with four types of people:

1) A Fāsiq (transgressor) - He will betray you for a morsel of food.

2) A liar - He will deceive you.

3) A foolish man - He will harm you even if he does something with a good intention.

4) A person who severs family ties - He is described as Mal'oon (accursed) in three places of the Holy Qur'ān."

Zainul Ābideen's ﷺ Du'ā

"O' Allāh ﷻ I seek Your protection from my outward appearance being pious to people while my heart is corrupt."

Zainul Ābideen's ﷺ Tolerance

Once a slave of Zainul Ābideen ﷺ was bringing a pot of steaming hot food from the stove for the guest. The pot accidently fell from the slave's hands onto Zainul Ābideen's ﷺ baby son. As a result of the accident, the child immediately died. Spontaneously Zainul Ābideen ﷺ set the slave free and commented, "He did not do it deliberately." He then commenced preparation for the Kafn (shroud) and Dafn (burial) of his son.

Zainul Ābideen's ﷺ Generosity

Once Zainul Ābideen ﷺ went to visit Muhammad Ibn Usāma. On seeing Zainul Ābideen ﷺ he broke down crying. When Zainul Ābideen ﷺ asked him for the reason of his grief, he replied that he was in debt.

Zainul Ābideen ﷺ asked, "How much is your debt?" Muhammad Ibn Usāma replied, "Fifteen thousand Dinār." Zainul Ābideen ﷺ said, "Payment of your debt is my responsibility."

The Fire of Ākhirah

Once the house of Zainul Ābideen ﷺ was on fire while he was in Salāh. The people shouted, "O son of Rasūlullāh ﷺ! Your house is on fire!"

However, Zainul Ābideen ﷺ was fully engaged in his Salāh. He was oblivious to the fire and the shouts of the people. He remained in Salāh until the fire died out. When people asked him about his obliviousness, he said, "The fire of the Ākhirah has made me oblivious to the fire of this world."

Who was Zainul Ābideen ﷺ?

Zainul Ābideen ﷺ was the son of Sayyidunā Husain ﷺ, who was the son of Sayyidunā Ali ﷺ, who was the son-in-law of Rasūlullāh ﷺ.

61

Thābit Ibn Nu'mān ﷺ

One of our pious predecessors, Thābit Ibn Nu'mān ﷺ, was hungry and tired as he was passing through a garden that bordered a river. He was so hungry to the extent that he could hear his stomach growling, and his eyes became focused on the fruits he saw on various trees of the garden. In a fit of desperation, he forgot himself and extended his hand to an apple that was within reach. He ate half of it and then drank water from the river. Then he became overcome by guilt, despite the fact that he had only eaten because of dire need. He said to himself, "Woe unto me! How can I eat someone else's fruits without his permission? I make it compulsory upon myself not to leave this place until I find the owner of this garden and ask him to forgive me for having eaten one of his apples."

After a brief search, he found the owner's house. He knocked on the door, and the owner of the garden came out and asked him what he wanted.

Thābit Ibn Nu'mān ﷺ said, "I entered your garden that borders the river, and I took this apple and I ate half of it. Then I remembered that it does not belong to me, so I ask you now to excuse me for having eaten it and to forgive me for my mistake." The man replied, "On one condition only will I forgive you for your mistake."

Thābit Ibn Nu'mān ﷺ asked, "And what is that condition?" He replied, "That you marry my daughter." Thābit ﷺ said, "I will marry her." The man said, "But heed to this, indeed my daughter is blind, she does not see, mute, she does not speak, deaf, she does not hear."

Thābit ﷺ began to ponder over his situation, a difficult predicament indeed did he find himself to be in now; what should he do? Do not get out of it, thought Thābit ﷺ, for he realised that to be tested by such a woman, to take care of her, and to serve her, are all better than to eat from the foul matter of the Hellfire as a recompense for the apple that he ate. And after all, the days of this world are few and limited.

And so he accepted the condition to marry the girl, seeking the reward from Allāh ﷻ. He was nonetheless somewhat anxious in the days prior to the marriage. He thought, how can I have relations with a woman who neither speaks nor sees nor hears? He became so miserable that he almost wished for the earth to swallow him up before the appointed date. Yet despite such apprehension, he placed his complete trust upon Allāh ﷻ, and he said, "There is neither might nor power except from Allāh ﷻ. Indeed to Allāh ﷻ do we belong, and to Him do we return." On the day of his marriage, he saw her for the first time. She stood up before him and said, "Peace be upon you and the mercy and blessings of Allāh ﷻ."

When he saw her grace and beauty, he was reminded of what he would see when he would imagine the fair maidens of Paradise. After a brief pause, he said, "What is this? She indeed speaks, hears and sees." He then told her what her father had said earlier.

She said, "My father has spoken the truth. He said I was mute because I do not speak any forbidden word, and I have never spoken to a man who is not lawful to me. And I am indeed deaf in the sense that I have never sat in the gathering in which there is backbiting, slander, or false and vain speech. And I am blind in the sense that I have never looked upon a man who is not permissible for me."

Dear readers! Reflect and learn a lesson from the story of this pious man and this pious woman and of how Allāh ﷺ brought them together. The fruit of this noble marriage was the birth of a child who grew up to fill the earth with knowledge; yes, their son was Imām Abū Haneefah Nu'mān, may Allāh ﷺ have mercy upon him.

Imām Abū Haneefah ﷺ
A Divine Foretelling

Sayyidunā Abū Hurairah ﷺ narrates, "We were present with the Holy Prophet ﷺ when, within this gathering, Sūrah Jumuah was revealed and the Holy Prophet ﷺ recited the following, **"Along with others of them who have not yet joined them."** (63:3)

The Companions thus enquired as to which people are referred to. The Holy Prophet ﷺ remained silent until he was asked again and then thrice. Sayyidunā Salmān Al-Fārsi ﷺ was amongst us. The Holy Prophet ﷺ placed his blessed hand on Salmān's shoulder saying, "If this sacred religion was placed on the Surayya star then without doubt from amongst his people there would surely be a particular individual or individuals who would rise to acquire this religion/faith." (Bukhāri, Muslim)

In relation to this Hadeeth, Imām Jalāl-ud-Deen Suyooti ﷺ and Imām Ibn Hajar Makki ﷺ stated that the statement of the Holy Prophet ﷺ, 'a particular individual' mentioned in the above Hadeeth is referring to our Imām Abū Haneefah ﷺ. The sole reason for them appointing this Hadeeth to Imām Abū Haneefah ﷺ was due to his determination and his deep rooted desire for this divine religion, and as no other Persian has such in-depth knowledge as Imām Abū Haneefah ﷺ.

Imām Sāhib's ﷺ Intelligence

Imām Abū Yūsuf ﷺ narrates that a man appeared before Imām Abū Haneefah ﷺ and submitted, "I buried some wealth in my house but I can't seem to recall exactly where I buried it."

Imām Sāhib ﷺ said, "How will I know where you buried it?" The moment the man heard this, he started weeping bitterly. Imām Sāhib ﷺ summoned his students and together with the man, they proceeded to his house. Imām Sāhib ﷺ asked him where his sleeping quarters were and where he kept his clothing etc. The man took them to a room of the house. Imām Sāhib ﷺ then asked his students, "If this house belonged to you and you had to bury something, where would you bury it in this room?" The students pin pointed five different places where they would have buried the item.

Imām Sāhib 🌸 asked them to start digging at those points. At the third point, his wealth was unearthed. Thereupon, Imām Sāhib 🌸 advised the man, "Express your gratitude to Allāh 🌸 for returning your wealth to you."

Go and Perform Salāh for the Entire Night

Hasan Ibn Ziyād 🌸 narrates that a man once buried some wealth but couldn't recall where he buried it. He searched for it but to no avail. When he came to Imām Abū Haneefah 🌸 and explained the situation to him. Imām Sāhib 🌸 asked him, "Is this some Fiqhi (juristic) problem that should be attended to by me? Okay, go and perform Salāh for the entire night and you will recall where you had buried it."

The man went home and at nightfall, he started performing Salāh. Not even a quarter of the night had passed when he recalled where he had buried it. He came back and informed Imām Sāhib 🌸 of the good news. Imām Sāhib 🌸 told him, "I knew Shaytān wouldn't allow you to perform Salāh for the entire night and he would make you recall the spot. Nevertheless, why didn't you spend the rest of the night in Salāh as an expression of gratitude to Allāh 🌸?"

A Wise Young Muslim Boy

Many years ago, during the time of the Tābi'een (the generation of Muslims after the Sahābah 🌼, Baghdad was a great city of Islām. In fact, it was the capital of the Islamic Empire and, because of the great number of scholars who lived there, it was the centre of Islamic knowledge.

One day, the ruler of Rome at the time sent an envoy to Baghdad with three challenges for the Muslims. When the messenger reached the city, he informed the Khaleefah (Caliph) that he had three questions which he challenged the Muslims to answer.

The Khaleefah gathered together all the scholars of the city and the Roman messenger climbed upon a high platform and said, "I have come with three questions. If you answer them, then I will leave with you a great amount of wealth which I have brought from the king of Rome." As for the questions, they were; "What was there before Allāh?", "In which direction does Allāh face?", "What is Allāh engaged in at this moment?"

The great assembly of people were silent. (Can you think of answers to these questions?) In the midst of these brilliant scholars and students of Islām was a man looking on with his young son. "O my dear father! I will answer him and silence him!" said the youth. So the boy sought the permission of the Khaleefah to give the answers and he was given the permission to do so.
The Roman addressed the young Muslim and repeated his first

question, "What was there before Allāh?" The boy asked, "Do you know how to count?" "Yes," said the man.

"Then count down from ten!" So the Roman counted down, "Ten, nine, eight,..." until he reached 'one' and he stopped counting.

"But what comes before 'one'?" asked the boy. "There is nothing before one - that is it!" said the man.

"Well then, if there obviously is nothing before the arithmetic 'one', then how do you expect that there should be anything before the 'One' Who is Absolute Truth, All-Eternal, Everlasting, the First, the Last, the Manifest, the Hidden?"

Now the man was surprised by this direct answer which he could not dispute. So he asked, "Then tell me, in which direction is Allāh facing?"

"Bring a candle and light it," said the boy, "and tell me in which direction the flame is facing?"

"But the flame is just light - it spreads in each of the four directions. North, South, East and West. It does not face any one direction only," said the man in wonderment.
The boy replied, "Then if this physical light spreads in all four directions such that you cannot tell me which way it faces, then what do you expect of the Noorus-Samāwāti-wal-Ardh: Allāh ﷺ - the Light of the Heavens and the Earth!? Light upon Light, Allāh ﷺ

faces all directions at all times."

The Roman was shocked and astounded that here was a young child answering his challenges in such a way that he could not argue against the proofs. So, he desperately wanted to try his final question. But before doing so, the boy said, "Wait! You are the one who is asking the questions and I am the one who is giving the answers to these challenges. It is only fair that you should come down to where I am standing and that I should go up where you are right now, in order that the answers may be heard as clearly as the questions."

This seemed reasonable to the Roman, so he came down from where he was standing and the boy ascended the platform. Then the man repeated his final challenge, "Tell me, what is Allāh doing at this moment?"

The boy proudly answered, "At this moment, when Allāh ﷺ found upon this high platform a liar and mocker of Islām, He caused him to descend and brought him low. And as for the one who believed in the Oneness of Allāh ﷺ, He raised him up and established the Truth. Every day, He exercises universal power."

The Roman had nothing to say except to leave and return back to his country, defeated. Meanwhile, this young boy grew up to become one of the most famous scholars of Islām. Allāh ﷺ, the Exalted, blessed him with special wisdom and knowledge of the Deen (religion). His name was Abū Haneefah ﷺ and he is known today as Imām-e-Ā'zam, the Great Imām and great scholar of Islām. May Allāh ﷻ shower His Mercy in the same way upon our Muslim children who are growing up today. Āmeen!

The Genius of Imām Abū Haneefah ﷺ

Imām Abū Haneefah ﷺ was one of the greatest genius minds of this Ummah. In addition to his vast command over Qur'ān and Hadeeth, he was also the person for any complex, mind puzzling situation which would be difficult to solve.

Once he was present in a Janāzah (funeral). The funeral was of a young Sayyid. Many great scholars were also participating. It so happened that suddenly the mother of the deceased appeared from nowhere and began crying and lamenting. She even went so far as to throw her head scarf upon the Janāzah. Her husband tried to calm her down but she would not listen. He became frustrated and said, "If you don't leave from here, I give you three Talāqs" (divorces). She in reply remarked, "If I return without participating in the Janāzah Salāh then all my properties are Sadaqah in the path of Allāh ﷻ." Those present had no idea how to resolve this situation. They turned towards Imām Abū Haneefah ﷺ. In response, he first ordered those lifting the Janāzah to put it down. He then ordered those who were walking ahead of the Janāzah to return. After this had been done, he ordered the father to lead the Janāzah Salāh in the middle of the road. After the Salāh he said to the lady, "Now you may return. Your vow is fulfilled and you will also not be separated from your husband."

Ibn Shubruma ﷺ said upon this, "Indeed women have been incapable of giving birth to someone of your liking."

(Tadhkiratun Nu'mān)

A Neighbour in Need

Imām Abū Haneefah ﷺ had a shoe maker as his neighbour. All day long the shoe maker sat at the door of his cottage and worked very hard making his shoes. And every night he drank and drank until he lost his senses and indulged in obscene songs and indecent noises that reached now and then even to the ears of the Imām who was engaged in meditation in the quiet corner of his house.

One night the Imām heard no noise coming from the shoe maker's cottage. He had a quiet night for divine meditation, but not a quiet mind.

Early next morning he hurried to the shoe maker's cottage, made anxious enquiry and came to learn that the police had taken away the drunkard to jail for his indecent behaviour.

The illustrious Caliph Mansūr was then at the head of the Muslim Empire. Great as the Caliph was, the Imām had never before treaded the steps of the Supreme Court. The Caliph himself occasionally appeared before his door. But today the danger of his

71

neighbour made the Imām restless and he at once left for the court.

The gate-keepers threw the door wide open and stepped aside in respect. The ministers of the court rubbed their eyes and the Caliph wondered and sprang forward. He made the saintly guest sit on his throne and enquired of the cause of his gracious visit.

The Imām said; "Your Majesty's police arrested a neighbour of mine last evening and lodged him in jail. I have come to intercede for his release, O Commander of the faithful!"

The Caliph paused for a moment and then replied: "Not only him, O great Imām, but for your honour, I hereby release all the prisoners of the jail!"

The Imām returned home with his neighbour. The neighbour never thereafter touched the wine-cup again.   (Seeratun-Numān)

Incidents of Intelligence

Imām Abū Haneefah ⬮ says, "I was with Ibn Hubayrah, (the ruler), who ordered my imprisonment. A deceptive person approached me and asked, "If the sultan orders someone to kill his fellow Muslim brother, is it permissible for him to kill that person?" Imām Sāhib ⬮ reversed the question and asked, "Was his killing necessary?" i.e. due to Qisās or some other reason. He said, "Yes." Imām Sāhib ⬮ replied, "Then he should kill him." He further asked, "What if the killing was not necessary?" Imām Sāhib ⬮ said, "The respected sultan can never give an order to kill an innocent person."   (Tadhkiratun Numān)

Abū Yūnus ⬮ reports: A person came to Imām Abū Haneefah ⬮ and said, "I had vowed never to speak to my wife unless she spoke to me first. She, in return, also took an oath saying, If I speak to you first then everything in my possession is Sadaqah (charity)." Imām Sāhib ⬮ asked if he had enquired of this Mas'alah from another Ālim. This person was a relative of Sufyān Thawri ⬮ and replied, "Yes, I asked Sufyān Thawri ⬮ who said "The oath of whoever speaks first will be broken, and will have to pay a penalty for breaking the oath." Imām Abū Haneefah ⬮ said. "Go and talk to your wife, neither of your oaths are broken." The person went to Sufyān Thawri ⬮ and informed him of Imām Abū Haneefah's ⬮ Fatwa. He was furious and came to Imām Abū Haneefah ⬮ and showed his anger. Imām Abū Haneefah ⬮ ordered the person to repeat his question and gave the same verdict. Sufyān Thawri ⬮ asked. "How can you give such an answer?" Imām Abū Haneefah

🌸 replied, "After he had made his vow and, in response, his wife took her oath 'she spoke to him,' therefore his vow is fulfilled. Now, when he talks to her, her vow will also be fulfilled."

Sufyān Thawri 🌸 was amazed and remarked, "These things just light up before you while we are left in darkness."

(Tadhkiratun Nu'mān)

A man once appeared before Imām Abū Haneefah 🌸 and enquired, "What is your opinion of a man who has no hope of Jannah, does not fear Jahannam, is not overcome with the fear of Allāh 🌸,consumes dead flesh, performs Salāh without Ruku or Sajdah, bears testimony to things he does not witness, dislikes Haq (truth), flees from the Rahmat (mercy) of Allāh 🌸, loves Fitnah (temptations) and gives testimony regarding the Jews and Christians?"

Imām Abū Haneefah 🌸 was quite aware that the man who posed the questions had hatred for him. He said, "You questioned me about issues, the answers of which you are quite aware of." The man submitted, "Yes, these are very immoral and major issues. There is nothing more evil than these beliefs. This is why I am asking you." Imām Sāhib 🌸 then directed the question to his students, "What is your opinion of a man with such attributes?" They all unanimously agreed, "He who possesses such attributes is the most evil person." Imām Sāhib 🌸 smiled and addressed the questioning man, "If I prove to you that this man is a saint, will you stop throwing abuses at me? Will you also refrain from forcing the angels on your shoulders to record things that are detrimental to you?" The man replied, "I accept that."

Imām Sāhib ﷺ said, " You said that this person has no hope of Jannah and does not fear Jahannam; this is because he has attached his hopes onto the owner of Jannah and fears the owner of Jahannam. You said that this person does not fear Allāh ﷻ; this is because he is well aware that Allāh ﷻ will never be unjust in His judgement. Allāh ﷻ Himself declares: **"And your Lord is not cruel to the servants"** (41:46)

You said that this person consumes dead flesh. He consumes fish (which is actually dead flesh). You said that this person performs Salāh without Ruku and Sajdah. Also, another meaning of Salāh is Durood (Salutations), therefore it could also imply that he is sending Durood upon the Holy Prophet ﷺ. You said that the person testifies to things he did not witness. This means he testifies to the Kalimah **"Lā Ilāha Illallāhu Muhammadur-Rasūlullāh"** You said that the person dislikes Haq (truth). This means he desires to live so that he may worship Allāh ﷻ to the utmost and he dislikes death because death is referred to as Haq as well. Allāh ﷻ says in the Holy Qur'ān **"And the pangs of death comes with Haq (truth)."** (50:19)

You said that this person loves Fitnah (temptations). So this means that he loves wealth and children. Allāh ﷻ says in the Holy Qur'ān **"Verily your wealth and your children are a Fitnah (temptation)."** (54:15)

You said that this person flees from the mercy of Allāh ﷻ. This means that he is fleeing from the rain (in fear that he gets drenched with it). You said this person gives testimony to the Jews and Christians. In fact he is giving testimony to this statement: **"The Jews claim that the Christians have nothing (to stand upon) and the Christians claim that the Jews have nothing (to stand upon)."**

(2:113)

He is actually verifying what both parties are claiming."

Upon hearing this discourse, the man got up and kissed Imam Sā-hib's ﷺ forehead. He then submitted, "You have spoken the truth. I bear witness to that."

Imām Abū Yūsuf ﷺ establishes his own circle of education

Khateeb Baghdādi ﷺ narrates, once when Imām Abū Yūsuf ﷺ, a senior student of Imām Abū Haneefah ﷺ fell ill, Imām Sāhib ﷺ went to visit him a number of times. On one occasion he found him looking very frail and weak. Imām Sāhib ﷺ recited Innā Lil-lāhi..... and remarked, "I hope you will remain after me for the benefit of the Muslims and if they are afflicted with your death, then a great treasure of knowledge will be terminated with your death."

According to another narration, Imām Sāhib ﷺ said, "If this young man dies, nobody on the entire face of the earth will be able to fill his place."

Imām Abū Yūsuf ﷺ was on his way to recovery, with the grace of

Allāh ﷻ, when he heard of the statement made by Imām Sāhib ﷺ. This created pride in his heart prompting him to establish his own circle of teaching. He eventually discontinued going to Imām Sāhib's ﷺ gathering. People also started turning towards him. Upon Imām Sāhib's ﷺ enquiry, he was informed that Imām Abū Yūsuf ﷺ had established his own circle when he heard of Imām Sāhib's ﷺ words of praises in his favour.

Imām Sāhib ﷺ summoned a reliable person and requested him to proceed to the gathering of Imām Abū Yūsuf ﷺ and pose the following question, "A man handed a garment to the laundryman with the belief that he will wash it for two Dirhams. When he went to collect the garment after a few days, the laundryman refused to acknowledge that he had ever received a garment from him. The man returned home and after a few days went back to the laundryman asking for his garment. The laundryman returned the washed garment to him. Now the question arises, is the laundryman eligible for the laundry fee or not?

Go and ask him (Abū Yūsuf ﷺ) this question. If he says that he is eligible, then tell him that he is wrong and if he says that he is not eligible then tell him that he is still wrong."

The man went to Imām Abū Yūsuf's ﷺ gathering and posed the question to him. Imām Abū Yūsuf ﷺ replied, "His fee is binding." The man replied, "You are mistaken." Imām Abū Yūsuf ﷺ puzzled over the issue for a little while, said, "No, he is not eligible for a fee."

77

The man again remarked, "You are mistaken." Immediately thereafter, Imām Abū Yūsuf ﷺ got up and proceeded to the Majlis of Imām Abū Haneefah ﷺ.

Imām Sāhib ﷺ asked, "It seems as though the issue of the laundryman has brought you here." He replied, "Yes." Imām Sāhib ﷺ commented, "Subhān-Allāh! A person who takes on the responsibility of issuing Fatāwa, establishes his own circle of teachings and speaks with authority in the Deen of Allāh ﷻ is in such a position that he is unable to issue a valid answer to a Mas'alah of Ijārah (contract)?"

Imām Abū Yūsuf ﷺ submitted, "My respected teacher! Please inform me of the correct answer." Imām Sāhib ﷺ replied, "If he washed the garment after he refused to hand it over, then he is not entitled to a fee because he washed it for himself. However, if he washed it before taking it, he is entitled to the fee because he washed it for the owner of the garment."

This is an inspiration from Allāh ﷻ

Abdullāh Ibn Mubārak ﷺ narrates: "I met Imām Abū Haneefah ﷺ en-route to Makkah Mukarramah. A calf was barbecued for all the companions travelling with him. His friends decided to consume the meat with vinegar but they were unable to find a utensil in which they could place the vinegar. A little later, they saw Imām Abū Haneefah ﷺ digging a hole in the sand and placing the table-cloth over the hole. He then put vinegar onto the cloth. The companions then ate the meat with vinegar by placing the meat onto the cloth. They then addressed Imām Sāhib ﷺ, "You do everything in a very pleasant manner." To this he replied, "Express your gratitude before Allāh ﷻ. This is something which Allāh ﷻ has inspired me to do."

The Distribution of the Deceased's Estate

Wak'ee Ibn Jarrāh ﷺ narrates, "I was sitting in the company of Imām Abū Haneefah ﷺ when a lady appeared before him and said, "My brother passed away leaving behind six hundred gold coins. However, I only received one coin from his estate." Imām Abū Haneefah ﷺ asked, "Who distributed the estate?" She replied, "Dāwood Tai." Imām Abū Haneefah ﷺ said, "You are entitled to this much only. Okay tell me, your brother left behind two daughters?" "Yes," she replied. "A mother as well?" "Yes." Imām Abū

Haneefah ﷺ asked, "He left behind a wife?" She replied, "Yes." "He left behind twelve brothers and one sister?" he asked. When she again replied in the affirmative, Imām Abū Haneefah ﷺ added, "The two daughters are entitled to two thirds of the estate and that amounts to four hundred coins. The mother will get one sixth which is one hundred coins and the wife will get one eighth which is seventy five coins. Twenty four of the remaining twenty five will go to the twelve brothers. Two coins for each one of them and the remaining coin will be your share."

The Tolerance of
Imām Abū Haneefah ﷺ

While he was busy teaching, a man once came up to Imām Abū Haneefah ﷺ and started to swear at him. When his students wanted to respond to the man, Imām Abū Haneefah ﷺ stopped them. Neither did he allow them to respond, nor did he say anything himself. After the lesson was completed and he was going home, the foolish man followed him and continued swearing at him. When he reached the door of his house, Imām Abū Haneefah ﷺ turned to the man and said, "This is the door to my house. If you have anything left to say, please say it now so that nothing is left in your heart." The man was embarrassed when he heard this and could give no reply. Because Imām Abū Haneefah ﷺ was an expert in the knowledge of Deen, he knew that it is not correct to reply to swears by swearing back.

Moral:

Neither did Imām Abū Haneefah 🌼 become upset by what the man was saying, nor did he say anything back to him. Instead he practiced tolerance because if he said anything, he would have become more upset and then the man would also have become angrier saying many more hurtful things. The behaviour of Imām Abū Haneefah 🌼 made the man embarrassed. Our elders say, "Silence can defeat a hundred people."

The Genius of Imām Abū Haneefah 🌼

On one occasion, Sufyān Thawri, Mis'ar Ibn Kidām, Mālik Ibn Mighwal, Ja'far Ibn Ziyād 🌼 and others were in a Waleemah ceremony. Imām Abū Haneefah 🌼 had also been invited. When all had gathered, the host appeared rather concerned and enquired about a dilemma which had befallen him. The people enquired about the nature of the problem. He requested that he wanted to keep it a secret. Imām Abū Haneefah 🌼 asked, "What is the problem?" He replied, "I wedded two of my sons with two sisters. Due to some mix up, they had been sent to the wrong girl." Imām Sāhib 🌼 asked, "Have they engaged in sexual intercourse?" He replied in the affirmative. Upon this Sufyān Thawri 🌼 remarked. "A similar case was brought before Sayyidunā Ali 🌼 whose verdict is enough for us. He had ordered that giving the dowry had become incumbent upon each of them because of the intercourse. Thereafter, each girl should complete the Iddah period (approximately three months) and then go to the original groom with whom their marriage was conducted. There will be no punishment for the mix-up.

The guests were listening attentively and were impressed by Sufyān's words.

Imām Abū Haneefah ﷺ sat silently. Mis'ar Ibn Kidām turned
towards him and asked, "Say something." Sufyān Thawri ﷺ said,
"What can he say?"

Imām Abū Haneefah ﷺ said, "Call upon both the grooms." When
they arrived he asked each of them; "Do you like the girl you slept
with?" They replied, "Yes." He asked, "What is the name of your
original bride who was with your brother?" He mentioned her
name. Imām Abū Haneefah ﷺ ordered him to divorce her. He then
did the same with the other groom. When they had both divorced
the one with whom their marriage was originally conducted, Imām
Abū Haneefah ﷺ recited the Khutbah of Nikāh and conducted the
Nikāh of each one of them with the girl who they had mistakenly
slept with (since their first marriages had not been completed, they
were under no obligation to sit for the period of Iddah. Therefore it
was permissible for them to remarry at once).

The guests were stunned at Imām Abū Haneefah's ﷺ verdict and
Mis'ar Ibn Kidām ﷺ stood up and kissed the forehead of Imām
Abū Haneefah ﷺ and exclaimed "People taunt me for my liking of
such a personality. Sufyān Thawri ﷺ sat quietly and he did not ut-
ter a word.   (Tadhkhiratun Nu'mān)

Stolen goods are recovered

Muhammad Ibn Hassān ﷺ narrates, "One night, a burglar broke into a man's house and got away with all his household goods. The burglar was from the very same street as well. Before the thief left the house, he compelled the house-owner to swear, 'If I tell any-body who the thief is, my wife will be divorced thrice.'

In the morning, the thief set out to sell the goods. The house-owner witnessed the scene but he could do nothing about it as he had sworn an oath. Overcome with anxiety, he appeared before Imām Abū Haneefah ﷺ and related the whole event. Imām Abū Haneefah ﷺ asked him to summon the Imām, Muazzin and other influential people of the street. When they all assembled before Imām Sāhib ﷺ, he asked them, "Do you want this man to recover all his stolen goods?" When they replied in the affirmative, Imām Sāhib ﷺ advised them, "Gather all the corrupt and evil people of the street in the Masjid or in a house. Thereafter, ask them to come out one by one. As they are coming out, ask this man if this is the culprit or not. If he is not the culprit, he should say so and if he is the culprit, then he should remain silent and you should then arrest him."

They did accordingly and with the grace of Allāh ﷺ he recovered all his stolen goods (and his wife was not divorced).

Imām Abū Haneefah's ﷺ Answer is the Most Correct

Fadl Sabkhuri ﷺ narrates Ibn Abi Layla ﷺ, Sufyān Thawri ﷺ, Shareek ﷺ and Imām Abū Haneefah ﷺ were all seated in a gathering when a man asked the following question, "A group of people are sitting when a snake fell onto one of them. He dusted the snake off himself and it landed onto a second person. He hurled it onto the third and the third hurled it onto the fourth person. The snake bit him and he ultimately died of its venom. The question now arises, who is responsible to pay the Diyyat (blood money)?"

All the members of the gathering started responding to the question. One of them said the first one was responsible whilst another said that all of them were responsible. Imām Sāhib ﷺ remained silent and smiling throughout the discussion. They eventually turned to him and said, "All of us have expressed our views on this issue. What is your view?"

Imām Sāhib ﷺ replied: "The first person hurled the snake onto the second person but the snake did not harm him. Hence, the first person is free of any blame. The same applies to the second and third person as well. As for the fourth person, if the snake did not bite him the moment it fell onto him, but bit him after a few moments, then the third person is also free of all blame. However, if it bit him the moment it fell onto him, then he (third person) is responsible."

The Understanding of
Imām Abū Haneefah ﷺ

"A man in Kufa believed Sayyidunā Uthmān ؓ was a Jew. When Imām Abū Haneefah ﷺ heard this, he went to his house. The man gave him a warm welcome. Imām Sāhib ﷺ told him, "I have brought a marriage proposal."

He asked, "For whom?" Imām Sāhib ﷺ replied, "For your young daughter." The man who seeks your daughter's hand is very noble and wealthy. He is a Hāfiz of the Holy Qur'ān. He spends the entire night in a single Rak'at of Salāh. He is also very generous. He weeps very bitterly out of fear of Allāh ﷻ.

The man exclaimed, "Imām Abū Haneefah, you didn't have to mention so many of his attributes. Less than that would have also sufficed." Imām Sāhib ﷺ then added, "However, there is one thing I did not mention." "What is that?" he asked. Imām Sāhib ﷺ replied, "The problem is that he is a Jew." The man retorted, "Subhān-Allāh! Are you suggesting I hand my daughter over to a Jew?" Imām Sāhib ﷺ replied, "Will you not hand her over then? He replied, "Never."

Upon this Imām Sāhib ﷺ remarked, "You are not prepared to marry your daughter off to a Jew whereas the Holy Prophet ﷺ got two of his daughters married to Sayyidunā Uthmān ؓ and according to your opinion he is a Jew. So if you won't give your daughter

85

in marriage to a Jew, do you think the Holy Prophet ﷺ will give two of his daughters to one?"

The man realised the wickedness of his belief and seeking forgiveness from Allāh ﷻ, he retracted what he had said.

Wisdom of Imām Abū Haneefah ﷺ

Imām Abū Haneefah ﷺ paid a visit to Madeenah where he was approached by Imām Bāqir ﷺ – who was one of the prominent scholars in Madeenah. Imām Bāqir ﷺ asked Imām Abū Haneefah ﷺ; "Are you the Imām Abū Haneefah who changed the Deen of my grandfather?" Imām Abū Haneefah ﷺ replied: "O Imām Bāqir! You have been misinformed about me. Sit down so that I can clear myself."

"Tell me, O Imām Bāqir ﷺ! Who is the weaker sex, the male or the female?" Imām Bāqir ﷺ replied: "The female." Imām Abū Haneefah ﷺ then asked: "Tell me of the male and female: what is the portion of their inheritance?" Imām Bāqir ﷺ replied: "For the male, two portions, and for the female, one portion." "O Imām Bāqir ﷺ!" said Imām Abū Haneefah ﷺ, "If I were to follow my own deduction, then I would have given two portions for the female and one portion for the male!"

Imām Abū Haneefah ﷺ (then) asked: "Which is greater Salāh or Saum (Fasting)?" Imām Bāqir ﷺ replied: "Salāh, of course." Imām Abū Haneefah ﷺ said: "If I were following my own desires as you have accused me of changing the Deen of your grandfather then I would have made Qadha of Salāh compulsory for the woman who is menstruating and not Qadha of fasting that she owes, seeing that we both agree that Salāh is greater than Saum."

By now, Imām Bāqir ﷺ was getting excited, and he said: "Tell me more." He was deeply impressed with Imām Abū Haneefah ﷺ. "Tell me, O Imām Bāqir! Which is more unclean: Semen or urine?" Imām Bāqir ﷺ replied "Urine is the more unclean of the two." Imām Abū Haneefah ﷺ said: "O Imām Bāqir! If I were to change the Deen of your grandfather Muhammad ﷺ then I would have made Ghusl (bath) compulsory after urinating and Wudhu necessary after ejaculation. I am only following the Deen of our Prophet Muhammad ﷺ." Upon hearing this, Imām Bāqir ﷺ was overjoyed and kissed the forehead of Imām Abū Haneefah ﷺ.

"If half the world's wisdom was to be put on one side of the scale and Imām Abū Haneefah's ﷺ wisdom on the other then the latter's wisdom would outweigh the former's."   (Ali Ibn Āsim)

Selflessness and Sacrifice of Imām Abū Haneefah ﷺ

In the latter period of Imām Abū Haneefah's ﷺ life, with age his body had become heavy, causing him difficulty in moving around. His house was situated on high ground, with a fair number of steps to climb to reach the entrance.

Imām Abū Haneefah 🌸 had just climbed up the steps and entered his house, and had just sat down with the intention of lying down to rest, when somebody called out to him from the bottom of the steps.

"I wish to ask you a question. Please come down!" Imām Abū Haneefah 🌸 came down and asked, "What is this question you wish to ask?" The person replied, "Oh, just as you reached the last steps I forgot." Imām Abū Haneefah 🌸 said, "It is of no consequence. When you remember you may ask," and Imām Sāhib 🌸 went back up the steps.

Just as Imām Sāhib 🌸 was about to lie down and rest, the same person called out again, "I have remembered! Come down!" Imām Sāhib 🌸 climbed down again. This time too it was the same story. The person said, "I had remembered but, just as you reached the last step I forgot."

Sometimes it was the last step that Imām Sāhib 🌸 had reached, sometimes it was the third or fourth step, but every time it was the same story, that he had remembered but had forgotten again.

In this way he had made Imām Sāhib 🌸 climb up and down six or seven times. Finally, when Imām Sāhib 🌸 had climbed down and enquired, "What is this question?" The person replied, "Yes! Yes! Now I remember!" Imām Sāhib 🌸 said, "Go ahead and ask." The person asked, "What is the taste of faeces?"

Let us pause for a moment here. He wanted to know what faeces tasted like, is this a question to put to anybody? How much trouble and inconvenience did he put Imām Sāhib ﷺ through to ask this question?

However, with an even temperament, with steadfastness and with a firm stance, Imām Sāhib ﷺ responded very calmly, "It depends. What type of faeces are you enquiring about - the taste of fresh faeces or the taste of stale faeces?"

The person replied, "Well…both! Tell me the taste of the fresh and the stale."

Imām Sāhib ﷺ answered, "The taste of fresh faeces is sweet and the stale is bitter."

The person asked, "What??? Did you taste each of them?"

Imām Sāhib ﷺ replied, "There is no necessity for one to taste each in order to determine these qualities. There are some signs of indication which will equally lead us to this conclusion. I have noticed that flies tend to settle on freshly passed faeces. Flies are attracted by sweetness. So one can conclude that freshly passed faeces are sweet. Flies do not settle on stale faeces. Bitterness repels flies." The person said, "What you have stated is absolutely cor-rect!" Imām Sāhib ﷺ in return asked him, "Why do you say so?" The person explained, "I knew the answers before hand."
He explained further, "We were a few people sitting together,

having a discussion and the question came up - 'In this present age, who is that person who is Sāhib-e-Ilm?' These people wanted to know who is the most accomplished in the quality of Ilm (knowledge), of selflessness, of giving sacrifice, of undergoing personal inconvenience for the sake of others. It was our unanimous opinion that it was Imām Abū Haneefah ﷺ. I came specifically to put you to the test, so that I could see for myself whether our unanimous opinion was correct!"

Subhān-Allāh! This is our beloved Imām Sāhib ﷺ, the great Imām! He is Nu'mān Ibn Thābit Ibn Zutā Ibn Marzubān, famously known as Imām Abū Haneefah ﷺ. He was born in the era of the Sahābah ﷺ in 80 A.H. in Kūfa, Irāq.

May Allāh ﷻ have mercy on his soul, enlighten his grave with His Noor and grant him a place in Jannah, Āmeen!

Valuable Advice of Imām Abū Haneefah ﷺ

We will relate some valuable advice of Imām Abū Haneefah ﷺ which he had given to his beloved son, Hammād.

Imām Abū Haneefah ﷺ said, "O my beloved son! May Allāh ﷻ keep your feet firm on guidance and be of assistance to you. I will give you some advices which, if you remember them and bring them into practice then I am hopeful that you will attain success in this world and the Hereafter:

1 - Adopt Taqwā, i.e. fear Allāh ﷻ, safeguard your limbs from sins and carry out His injunctions. In this manner bring alive the Ibādah of Allāh ﷻ.

2 - Those things which are necessary for you to know never remain ignorant of them.

3 - Never associate with anyone except to fulfil a worldly or Deeni need.

4 - Pay special attention to fulfilling the rights of others and never ask for your rights to be fulfilled except in dire need.

5 - Don't harbour enmity, neither for a Muslim or non-Muslim.

6 - Be satisfied and content with the wealth and status which Allāh ﷻ has bestowed on you.

7 - In order to be independent of others, you should fulfil your own tasks with proper means and good planning.

8 - Don't make yourself the object of others' gaze.

9 - Don't involve yourself in futile talk and play.

10 - When meeting others, be the first to make Salām. Speak good

things and associate with only the good and refrain from the evil.

11 - Engage in excessive Dhikr of Allāh 🅰 and Durood Shareef.

12 - Always recite Istighfār in the same words as reported by the Holy Prophet 🅰. He who recites it during the evening and passes away during the night will attain Jannah, and if he recites it in the morning and passes away during the day then too he will attain Jannah.

13 - Recite the Holy Qur'ān in abundance and convey the reward unto the Holy Prophet 🅰, your parents, teachers and all Muslims.

14 - Be more wary of your associates than you are of your enemies, because these are trying times, and it is our friends who become our enemies.

15 - Keep your secrets, capital, plans and travels hidden.

16 - Keep good relations with your neighbours & maintain patience on whatever harm they may cause you.

17 - Remain on the path of the Ahlus-Sunnah wal-Jamā'at and save yourself from the way of the ignorant ones.

18 - Keep a clean and sincere intention in all your works and always earn a Halāl sustenance.

19 - Practise the following five Ahādeeth which I have extracted

from 500,000:

- "A goodness of one's Islām is that he abandons futile things."

- "None of you can be a complete Muslim until he loves for his Muslim what he loves for himself."

- "Halāl is clear and Harām is clear and whatever is in between these two is doubtful, of which many people are unaware. He who saves himself from doubtful things has safeguarded his Deen and chastity. He who indulges in doubtful things will soon indulge in Harām, just like that sheep which grazes on the border. Soon it will trespass and eat from the other pasture. Beware! Every king has his restrictions and the restrictions of Allāh ﷺ are those things He has made Harām. Know! That there is a piece of flesh in every man which, if it is protected then the entire body will be protected and if it is spoilt then the entire body will be spoilt. Know! That flesh is the heart."

- "A true Muslim is he from whose hand and tongue others are safe."

- "You should suspend your good times (youth) between hope and fear. When death nears, then you should have hope in Allāh ﷺ and die hoping in His mercy, because indeed He is Most Forgiving and Most Merciful."

Imām Mālik 🕊

Imām Mālik 🕊 was born in Madeenah in 93 Hijri corresponding to 712 A.D. He remained in Madeenah for all his life, and the city influenced the school named after him, the Māliki School (Arabic: Mālikiyyah). His household was known to be one of knowledge, especially the study of Prophetic narrations (Ahādeeth). The books of history state that Imām Mālik's 🕊 grandfather, Mālik Ibn Abi 'Amr, was a great scholar of Hadeeth who narrated from the Companions.

During his life, Madeenah was the centre of Islamic learning. This was the city where the majority of legal rulings were revealed. The implementation of the Holy Qur'ān and Sunnah (the Shari'ah), continued in the city of Madeenah during the times of the Rightly-Guided Caliphs, Sayyidunā Abū Bakr 🕊, Sayyidunā Umar 🕊 and Sayyidunā Uthmān 🕊. The great Companion, Sayyidunā Abdullāh Ibn Mas'ood 🕊 would give a fatwa (legal ruling) about a matter in Iraq; but if he found that the ruling in Madeenah was different, he would leave his opinion.

Al-Muwatta and the Principles of Imām Mālik 🕊

Although the Imām wrote a number of books, his most famous work is Al-Muwatta, a work containing thousands of Ahādeeth and sayings from the Companions 🕊 and their students. The Imām described his methodology to this work in the following term:

"Most of what is in the book is my opinion but, by my life, it is not mere opinion since I heard it from more than one person from the people of knowledge and excellence and the Imāms who are followed from whom I took knowledge. They are the ones who had great fear of Allāh ﷻ. It became too repetitive for me (to mention all that), so I said, 'my opinion'. My opinion is the same as the opinion of the Companions, which they found with them and subsequently I found with them. This is an inheritance which has passed on from generation to generation down to our time. So it is the opinion of the previous Imāms."

Imām Suyooti ﷺ in his introduction to Tanweerul-Hawālik, quoted Imām Shāfi'ee's ﷺ statement, "After the Book of Allāh ﷻ, there is no book on the face of the earth more authentic than the book of Imām Mālik."

After the Holy Qur'ān and the Sunnah, Imām Mālik ﷺ considered the 'Practice of the People of Madeenah' to be a foundational principle upon which legal rulings were to be based. In fact, he was not the first Imām to support this method; Rabee'a ﷺ, Imām Mālik's first Shaykh in Jurisprudence, said, "A thousand from a thousand is better than one from me." (Meaning that the collective practice of Islām amongst the people of Madeenah, who learnt the religion from the Companions is stronger than following a narration which has only been passed down from one narrator to another narrator). Imām Mālik ﷺ himself said, "The learned among the Followers quoted Hadeeth which had been conveyed to them from others and they said, "We are not ignorant of this, but the common practice is different.'"

This matter of following the 'Practice of the people of Madeenah" was to become a point which Imām Shāfi'ee ﷺ, the great student of Imām Mālik ﷺ would come to disagree with; which is a legitimate difference of opinion between two qualified jurists and is not a cause of concern for the unqualified, who have only been called upon by the jurist of history to follow one school only of a qualified jurists, in obedience to the Qur'anic verse, **"So ask the people of knowledge if you do not know" (16:43)**

Imām Mālik's ﷺ Manners and Rank

Due to the deep love of Madeenah, he never rode in the city. He did not give Fatwa until 70 Shaykhs (scholars) of Madeenah testified that he was ready to give Fatwa. When he taught, he was serious and did not consider light-heartedness appropriate for a student of knowledge, although in private gatherings, which were not strict lessons of religious instructions, he would be cheerful with the students and others. He often said, "I don't know," and would finish a Fatwa.

Imām Shāfi'ee ﷺ said, "When a Hadeeth comes to you from Imām Mālik ﷺ, hold onto it tightly... When Scholars are mentioned, know that Imām Mālik ﷺ is a star. No one reached the level that Imām Mālik ﷺ did in knowledge through his memory, his proficiency and his piety. Whoever wants sound Hadeeth must have Imām Mālik."

The great Imām passed away in 179 Hijri corresponding to 795

A.D; and Allāh 🕮 gave success to his teachings and he became one of the 'four Imāms', whose teachings Allāh 🕮 spread throughout the lands. No-one has reached the rank of these Imāms, (May Allāh 🕮 illuminate their resting places) – since their time, which is why great Imāms of Hadeeth such as Tahāwi, Qādi 'Iyād, Nawawi and 'Asqalāni have followed these Imāms; not due to mere blind imitation, but rather as a realisation that these people were more qualified than themselves to understand, directly, the Holy Qur'ān and Sunnah; which is a humility which the present Muslim has a great difficulty in internally accepting. As the great Hadeeth scholar, Shaykh Shu'ayb Arna'ut said: "They (the Imāms of the four schools) are explainers, not popes, but in each of their schools there afterwards followed a hundred or more scholars who refined and added to their work, men whose status in Islamic knowledge was like mountains, any of whom could put fifteen of the scholars available today in his pocket."

Imām Shāfi'ee 🕮
(150 AH - 204 AH)

Imām Shāfi'ee 🕮 is one of those great personalities in the history of Islām from whom the Ummah has benefited from until the present day. Imām Shāfi'ee 🕮 was born to a poor family in Yemen. He was deprived of fatherly affection from a very young age. His mother took him from Yemen to Makkah Mukarramah. How was his education to begin here?

An orphan from a poor background had no real means of engaging in any sort of Ta'leem (education). Imām Shāfi'ee ﷺ says, "I passed my youth as an orphan in my mother's care. My mother had nothing to offer my teacher. I would attain the teacher's pleasure by overseeing the other children during his absence."

He had no access to paper to write on. He had a small bag by him. He would write on clean bones and place them in his bag. At nights he had no means of light in his home, so he would go and write his notes under the state lamps nearby.

In order to learn the Arab culture and grammar, he spent a period of time going around the Arab villages, where he reached perfection in Arabic genealogy, poetry and grammar.

Most people were aware of the genealogy of men, but one day some people came to him and enquired about the genealogy of women. Imām Shāfi'ee ﷺ sat with them and explained the entire night, and only ceased the next morning.

Allāh ﷻ had instilled in him the love for Ilm (knowledge). Someone once asked him how much he loved Ilm, to which he replied, "When any new knowledge falls to my ears, then all the limbs in my entire body desire to keep it memorised."

He was asked how much of greed he has for acquiring knowledge, to which he replied, "As much as a very greedy person has for wealth."

He was asked what his condition was in searching for knowledge to which he replied, "The same condition as the search of a mother who has lost her only child, would undergo."

He used to say, "The value of the person who learns the Holy Qur'ān increases; whoever discusses Fiqh, his worth increases; whoever writes down Hadeeth, his testimony becomes strong; whoever engages in reckoning, his opinion is strengthened; and he who does not protect his Nafs achieves no benefit from his knowledge."

He would never eat to his fill. Once he ate to his fill and vomited the food out. He would say, "Eating to one's fill makes the body weighty, the heart remains heavy, one's alertness and intellect is diminished and sleep overcomes one."

He kept a regular pattern for the nights. One third he would spend in writing, the second in Ibādah (worship) and the third in resting. It was his habit to complete the Holy Qur'ān sixty times during the month of Ramadhān. He would emphasise greatly on not wasting one's time in futility and unnecessary works. He would say that abstention from futility would result in the heart exuding a Noor (light). He would also encourage people to remain in isolation and not to intermingle. He would stress on eating less and would say that excessive eating leads to sleepiness. He greatly prohibited socialising with ignorant people.

He used to encourage asking the scholars every type of question, because, he used to say, if one knows the Mas'alah, then it will strengthen one's knowledge and if one did not know it, then it will be an addition to one's knowledge. He had an aversion for fame and would always comment that he wished that people read and benefited from the Kitābs (books) he wrote; but that they did not connect the Kitābs to him (i.e. he wished to remain anonymous).

During his last illness, Imām Muzni 🏵 said that he visited Imām Shāfi'ee 🏵 and asked regarding his health. Imām Shāfi'ee 🏵 replied, "I am about to bid farewell to my brothers. I do not know whether the abode of my soul will be Jannah, so that I may congratulate it, or whether it will be Jahannam so that I may mourn it." He then started crying and recited a poem, whose meaning is as follows:

When my heart hardens and my
desires get constrained, I have laid my
hopes on Your forgiveness.

I know well my sins but O' Rabb, when
I compare it to Your forgiveness then the
latter is much more greater.

If you take me to task for my sins, then too
I will not lose hope on Your mercy, even though I am deserving of
Jahannam due to my sins.

I am well aware of the multitude of my sins, but I also know well
that Allāh 🏵 is
Forgiving and Merciful.

100

Imām Ahmad Ibn Hanbal ﷺ

His Birth & Life:

Imām Ahmad ﷺ was born on 164/780, in Baghdad. Shaykh Abū Zahrah ﷺ mentions that the Imām experienced five things, which can lead one onto distinction: noble lineage; orphaned from a young age; self-reliance; self-control; and experience of adversity. The Imām was content and keen of intellect; an intellect fired with the fear of Allāh ﷻ and the belief that only Allāh ﷻ can bring harm or benefit to one. Moreover, he was abstinent; as illustrated by the fact that when Al-Mutawakkil offered him wealth, he returned it in humility.

The Imām was studious from a young age. Now, during this time in Baghdad, the science of the sacred Law (Shari'ah) were two: the field of Fiqh (legal jurisprudence) and the field of Hadeeth (Prophetic narrations). Imām Ahmad ﷺ chose the latter in the initial stages of his education. His first teacher was Imām Abū Yūsuf ﷺ, the student and colleague of Imām Abū Haneefah ﷺ. The Imām mentioned, "The first thing I wrote was the Ahādeeth of Imām Abū Yūsuf ﷺ." After being with Imām Abū Yūsuf ﷺ, he studied Hadeeth for four years with the Traditionalists (Muhaddithoon) of Baghdad, Haitham Ibn Basheer ﷺ; and, during the same period, he studied with Abdur-Rahmān Ibn Mahdi, Abū Bakr Ibn Āliyah and other famous Hadeeth Scholars. Once he had studied in Baghdad, he set out for Basra, Hijāz, Yemen, Syria and Al-Jazeerah, where he continued his specialisation in Hadeeth. He was also a student of Imām Shāfi'ee ﷺ; and the latter trusted Imām

Ahmad Ibn Hanbal's ﷺ proficiency in Hadeeth to such an extent that he said to Imām Ahmad ﷺ, "If you consider the Hadeeth sound, tell me and I will take it, be it Hijāzi, Syrian, Iraqi or Yemeni."

Shaykh Abū Zahrah ﷺ quotes Ibn Jawzi ﷺ as saying, "Imām Ahmad ﷺ did not set himself up to transmit Hadeeth and give Fatwa until he was forty years old." Before this time arrived, he was already famous in the Ummah; therefore his lessons were very crowded from the beginning. Shaykh Abū Zahrah ﷺ states that some historians have mentioned that 5000 people attended, with 500 narrators of what was transmitted. One of the students of Imām Shāfi'ee ﷺ quoted the Imām saying, "When I left Baghdad , I did not leave behind anyone more steadfast or god-fearing, or with more Fiqh than Ahmad Ibn Hanbal."

When the Imām died in 241 A.H., the whole city of Baghdad turned out. Historians have noted that 800,000 men and 60,000 women attended his funeral.

His Works and School of Law:

Imām Ahmad ﷺ did not pass on any books of Fiqh, so the Ummah has had to rely upon the reports of his students with regards to his statements on matters of Sacred Law (Shari'ah). What is famous from Imām Ahmad ﷺ himself, is his Musnad, a Hadeeth collection consisting of 30,000 Hadeeth. This work covers a vast range of subjects. This book is famous due to Ahmad Ibn Hanbal ﷺ, his articulation of any difference that arose in a narration from different narrators; the work also served as a resource for work on theology and Arabic language. Muhammad Siddiqi points out that the work became less popular as other 'better planned more practical' works of Hadeeth emerged in the third and fourth Muslim centuries. Nevertheless, the work has maintained a level of 'sanctity' amongst the Muslims due to the reverence that the Muslims held for the Imām, because of his defence of truth, when the Rationalists (Mu'tazilah) gained control of the caliphate, and Imām Ahmad 🙵 stood up and spoke the truth to the ruler, when nobody else did; a feat which led to the Imām spending 28 months in imprisonment, whilst getting lashed. This action of the Imām was so brave and so solitary, at a time when one risked one's life for the sake of speaking the truth in the face of falsehood, that the great Muhaddith, 'Ali Ibnul-Madeeni 🙵, said, "Allāh 🙵 had entrusted the defence of Islām to two people whom no one can emulate: one was Sayyidunā Abū Bakr Siddeeq 🙵 on the occasion of the apostasy, while the other was Ahmad Ibn Hanbal 🙵 during the calamity of the creation of the Qur'ān."

His Character:
He was steadfast in following the Sunnah, as well as a possessor of wonderful manners. Shaykh Abū Zahrah 🙵 states that he was poor, and he would work for a living, thus ensuring for lawfulness of his food and allowing him to stay away from gifts, which he refused. He was also patient and steadfast, as highlighted when he was persecuted for defending Ahlus-Sunnah points of Orthodoxy. Shaykh Abū Zahrah 🙵 said that he believed that the Imām's great steadfastness came about because Allāh 🙵 was supporting him,

and his reliance was upon Him only, in that he only felt the power of Allāh ﷻ and no one else. He was incredibly sincere and never sought fame; he once said, "I would like to settle in Makkah where I could lose myself in one of the narrow valleys and so escape being recognised." Moreover, he commanded great awe. One contemporary said, "I visited Ishāq Ibn Ibrāheem and other rulers, but I did not see anyone who inspired more awe than Imām Ahmad Ibn Hanbal ﷺ. I went to speak to him about something and I began to tremble from awe when I saw him."

In Al-Manāqib, it is related from a contemporary of the Imām, "I did not see anyone in the time of Ahmad who more combined religiousness, chastity, self-control, good manners and noble character, a firm heart, generous, noble companionship and lack of laziness than him." Another person said, "Ahmad was the most modest and noblest of the people. He had the best manners. He often bowed his head and lowered his eyes. Only discussion of Hadeeth was heard from him. He mentioned the righteous and the saints with gravity, tranquillity and fine words. When he met anyone, he smiled at them and welcomed them. He was very humble towards scholars and honoured and respected them."

Conclusion:
Like all the great scholars of Islām, Imām Ahmad's ﷺ greatness steamed from his character being based on the guidance of the Holy Prophet ﷺ. Although Imām Ahmad ﷺ was a great Hadeeth Scholar, who had memorised 100,000 Hadeeth, in terms of text (matn) and chain (isnād), his religion was not just about narration;

rather, he implemented the religion, and had become a man who practised what he knew, and Allāh ﷺ raised his rank so that people from the East to the West would still be admiring the virtues of this great man until this day.

Is there Such an Example?

The teacher wrote to his obedient and dutiful student that he desired to meet him so he should come to his house. The dutiful student immediately abandoned all his work and tasks and set off for his teacher. When he arrived he sat down with utmost respect and took the Du'ās of his teacher. The teacher's desire of meeting his student was fulfilled.

The teacher had earlier told his family that an obedient and dutiful student of his would be arriving shortly and that he was a pious student who always performed Tahajjud Salāh. His household prepared a variety of dishes in expectation of this student.

After having completed the meal they set off for the Masjid for Ishā Salāh. At home the daughter of the house folded the Dastarkhān (table cloth) and placed water and a prayer mat for the guest in readiness for his Tahhajjud Salāh. This was done for his convenience so that when he wakes up in the night, he is not in any difficulty.

After the teacher and his student completed Ishā Salāh, they returned home and both of them retired to their respective quarters to rest for the night.

The night passed and both of them set off for Fajr Salāh the next morning. The daughter went to the guest quarters and noticed that the water and the prayer mat were untouched. She was greatly surprised.

After Salāh the host and the guest returned home. The host entered the house and his daughter came up to him and asked, "Dear father, you have told us that this student of yours is very pious but last night he ate to his fill, where as he should have eaten only a little so that he may engage in Ibādah at night. Secondly, it appears that he had slept the whole night through and not awoken for Tahajjud Salāh, because he had not used any of the preparations we had left for him. Thirdly, it seems as though he left for Fajr Salāh without even making Wudhu. Tell me are these all not matters of great concern?"

The teacher listened attentively to what his daughter had told him and proceeded towards his guest to explain the great concerns.

The guest explained regarding his actions during that night saying, "Respected teacher, I intended keeping all this a secret but since you have asked me about it, I need to divulge it to you. The reason why I ate to my fill is because when I placed the first morsel in my mouth, I found it to be so blessed that I cannot explain in words, these blessings lead me to eat to my fill. My consumption of your Halāl and wholesome food had lead me to spend the entire night contemplating over a single verse of the Holy Qur'ān. I spent the entire night until it was time for Fajr contemplating on this verse from which I had deduced many Masā'il. Since I was so engrossed in this one verse I didn't get the opportunity to perform my Tahajjud Salāh. I still had my Wudhu from Ishā Salāh, therefore I did not see the need to renew it at the time of Fajr which explains why the water was left untouched."

That's right! These are the fruits and benefits of Halāl sustenance, where in one night many Masā'il were deduced from one single verse. What a blessed era that was! What Allāh 🕮 fearing people they were! What high status of knowledge they had! This incident is only an example of their virtue. The teacher was none other than Imām Shāfi'ee 🕮 and the student was Imām Ahmad Ibn Hanbal 🕮.

With the passing of time, teachers and students of that calibre are quickly diminishing. Nowadays you will hardly find the like thereof. The ability to deduce and make Ijtihād like they used to do is unheard of today, so too is that Halāl and wholesome sustenance which they earned.

Today, knowledge is only acquired for name and fame. Even after spending the whole night in sleep it becomes difficult to wake up for Fajr Salāh! Halāl sustenance is also lacking in our society. There is no benefit in Harām sustenance that merely snatches away blessings and progress.

Imām Abū Yūsuf ﷺ
(113 AH - 182 AH)

"Knowledge does not give any part of itself to you, until you give your full self to it."

The above is the statement of Yaqūb Ibn Ibrāheem Al-Ansāri Al-Kūfi ﷺ, who is famously better known as Imām Abū Yūsuf ﷺ or Qādhi Abū Yūsuf ﷺ.

He was born in the year 113 A.H. His father passed away whilst he was still young. Ali Ibn Ju'd ﷺ says that he used to hear Imām Abū Yūsuf ﷺ saying: My father passed away whilst I was still young and my mother used to send me to the washer-man to work, but I would go and sit in the gathering of Imām Abū Haneefah ﷺ. My mother would follow me and take me away from Imām Sāhib's ﷺ gathering and leave me at the washer-man.

I would again go and sit in Imām Sāhib's ﷺ gathering. This continued for some time, when one day my mother approached Imām Sāhib ﷺ and complained to him, "This is an orphan. Besides him I have none to support me and I live off what he earns. You have estranged him."

Imām Sāhib ﷺ replied, "This boy will acquire (great) knowledge. And soon he will be partaking of Falooda from plates of Fairooz."

Listening to this, his mother commented, "You are certainly in old days."

Imām Abū Yūsuf 🌸 states that after he had become the Qādhi, he was one day sitting in the company of Hāroon Rasheed, when they were served Falooda in Fairooz plates. The Khaleefah asked him to taste it because it was a dish rarely made by them. Imām Abū Yūsuf 🌸 asked, "What is this?" The Khaleefah replied, "This is Falooda."

Imām Abū Yūsuf 🌸 says that when he heard this he started smiling. When the Khaleefah asked the reason for his smile, he related the entire incident to him.

The Khaleefah commented that indeed knowledge benefits in both, this world and the Hereafter.

May Allāh 🌸 have mercy on Imām Abū Haneefah 🌸 who saw with the eyes of his heart which the physical eyes could not notice.

Imām Abū Yūsuf 🌸 was the most senior of judges in his era. He was even entitled, the Chief Justice of this World. He was the deputy Khaleefah in all those places over which the Khaleefah ruled.

Imām Abū Haneefah 🌸 used to say that Imām Abū Yūsuf 🌸 was the most knowledgeable of all his companions.

Ibn Sama'a 🌸 said, "After attending to the duty of Justice, Imām Abū Yūsuf 🌸 would perform 200 Rakāts of Salāh everyday."

Many great and prominent personalities would come and sit in his gatherings, luminaries such as Imām Ahmad Ibn Hanbal ☼ and Imām Muhammad Ibn Hasan ☼.

The Justice of Qādhi Abū Yūsuf ☼

Imām Abū Yūsuf ☼ would exercise the greatest level of justice and precaution in executing his duty. He describes this in his own words:

"I have hope in Allāh ☼ that after He has deputed me with the duty of being a judge, He will not question me about being oppressive to any party or being biased towards anyone. I have, however fear that He may take me to task regarding one particular incident. A person came to me and claimed that an orchard of his was in the control of Ameerul-Mu'mineen Hāroon Rashīd. I asked Ameerul-Mu'mineen regarding this and he replied that the orchard was his and it was sold to him by Khaleefah Mahdi. I told the claimant, "You have heard the reply of Ameerul-Mu'mineen, what have you to say?"

He asked Ameerul-Mu'mineen to take an oath, and he refused. I told him that I will ask him thrice to take an oath and if he does then, fine otherwise I will have to make a ruling in favour of the claimant.

I asked Ameerul-Mu'mineen thrice to take an oath and he refused. I eventually passed the ruling in favour of the claimant. I now fear that Allāh ﷻ will take me to task on this issue and ask me why I had not meted out justice."

Countless people have benefited from Imām Abū Yūsuf ﷫, Imām Muhammad Ibn Hasan ﷫, Imām Ahmad Ibn Hanbal ﷫, Bishr Ibn Waleed ﷫, Yahyā Ibn Ma'een ﷫, Ali Ibn Ju'd ﷫ and Amr Ibn Abi Amr ﷫.

He passed away in the year 182 AH at the age of 69. Bishr Ibn Ghawāth ﷫ said that he heard Imām Abū Yūsuf ﷫ say, "I accompanied Imām Abū Haneefah ﷫ for 17 years and then I was appointed to the mantle of justice for 17 years and now I deem my appointed time is near."

Bishr Ibn Ghawāth ﷫ says that a few months thereafter, Imām Abū Yūsuf ﷫ passed away.

The Fruits of Sincerity and Honesty

Mubārak Abū Abdullāh ﷫ worked for a long time in an orchard. The orchard belonged to a trader who one day called Mubārak ﷫ and asked him, "O Mubārak! Go and get me a sweet pomegranate."

Mubārak ﷫ went and plucked off a pomegranate from a tree and brought it to his master. The man cut it open but found that it was extremely bitter.

111

"Mubārak!" he shouted, "I asked for a sweet pomegranate and you have brought me a bitter one! Please go and get me a sweet one!"

Mubārak ﷺ went to another tree and fetched another pomegranate. When the master cut this one, he found to his disappointment that it was also very bitter.

"Don't you know the difference between a sweet and a bitter pomegranate?" he asked.

"I am sorry, my master," Mubārak ﷺ said, "But I have never tasted a single pomegranate in this orchard. I do not know which tree grows sweet ones and which tree grows bitter ones."
The master asked in surprise, "You have never eaten a single fruit from this orchard?!"

He replied, "You have employed me to care for the fruits and not to eat them. I have therefore never eaten a single fruit because I have no permission to do so."

The trader was surprised and also pleased to know that he was a very honest man.

The trader had a daughter who he wished to get married. Although many people proposed for her hand in marriage, he did not marry her to anyone.

He therefore called Mubārak ﷺ one day and asked him, "As you know, I have a daughter who is receiving marriage proposals. However, it is difficult for me to decide who to marry her to. I therefore wish to ask for your advice."

Mubārak ﷺ replied, "During the time of ignorance, people looked for a man with high family lineage to marry their daughters to. The people of other religions however look for wealth and beauty. In our religion, we give importance to the condition of a person's Islām."

The trader was impressed by Mubārak's ﷺ intelligence and said to his wife, "I see no one better than Mubārak to marry our daughter to. He is extremely honest and reliable and earns a Halāl income." He therefore married his daughter to Mubārak ﷺ and out of this marriage the great saint and scholar Abdullāh Ibn Mubārak ﷺ was born.

Eight Lessons of Hātim Asamm ﷺ

Hātim Asamm ﷺ was a renowned Sufi and a favourite pupil of Shaqeeque Balki ﷺ. Once the Shaykh asked him, "Hātim, how long have you been in my company?" He replied, "Thirty-three years." The Shaykh said, "What did you learn during these thirty-three years of association with me?" Hātim ﷺ replied, "I have learnt eight lessons." At this Shaqeeque ﷺ, out of disappointment, recited: Innā lillāhi wa innā ilayhi rājioon (Indeed We are Allāh's ﷺ and indeed unto Him are we returning).
He said regretfully, "You learnt only eight lessons during long

years of association with me? I have wasted all my life in association with you?" The Shaykh said, "Tell me, what are those eight lessons?"

Hātim ﷺ answered thus:

1. I have found that everybody loves someone or something, but I know that, as soon as he is laid in the grave, his loved ones part company with him. Consequently, I have cultivated love for good deeds so that when I die and pass into the grave, my good deeds should also accompany me into the grave and I should not be left alone.

2. I have read in the Holy Qur'ān that Allāh ﷺ says: **"But as for him who feared (in this world) to stand before his Lord (in the Hereafter) and restrained himself from (unlawful indulgence in) lust, Indeed Jannah will be his home."** (An Nāzi'āt: 40-41)
I know whatever Allāh ﷺ says is true. Therefore, I have restrained myself from unlawful desires and I have become steadfast in devotion to Him.

3. I know that in this world, things which are dearest and most precious to men are preserved with great care and protected with diligence. Allāh ﷺ says: **"That which you have (in the world) is destroyed (either you die and leave it behind or it will be wasted away in your life and that which Allāh ﷺ has, remains"** (eternally). **(An-Nahl: 96)**
Accordingly, whenever I came by something which was of great value to me, or which I prized above other things, I spend it for the

cause of Allāh ﷻ (give it in Allāh's ﷻ care), so that it should be preserved forever.

4. I have observed that for honour and glory, men turn to wealth, nobility of parentage and other things of pride, but Allāh ﷻ says: **"Indeed the noblest of you in the sight of Allāh is the best in piety."** (Al-Hujurāt:13) I therefore have cultivated piety in myself so that I should become the noblest of people in the sight of Allāh ﷺ.

5. I have noticed that people abuse others, revile them or find fault with them out of jealousy. Then I read in the Holy Qur'ān: **"We have apportioned amongst people their livelihood in the life of the world, and (in this apportionment) We have raised some of them above others in rank, (so) that some of them (should) take labour from others."** (Az-Zukhruf:32) Therefore, I have restrained myself from jealousy and ceased to concern myself with other people's affairs. I know for certain that the distribution of livelihood is entirely in the Hands of Allāh ﷻ and He grants as much as He pleases to whomsoever He likes. I have realised that a man's personal effort has little to do with his prosperity or adversity.

6. I have observed that in this world, everybody is hostile to someone or the other, and Allāh ﷻ says in the Holy Qur'ān: **"Indeed Shaytān (the devil) is an enemy for you, so treat him as an enemy (Do not be friends with him) (Al-Fātir:6)** So I have directed all my hostilities against Shaytān alone and I always try to keep away from him by all possible means. And as Allāh ﷺ has

115

commanded us to treat him as an enemy, I bear no enmity against anyone other than Shaytān.

7. I have observed that all people are struggling hard to seek their livelihood, so much so that they disgrace themselves before others and adopt unlawful means for obtaining their daily bread. However, Allāh ﷻ says: **"And there is no living being that moves on the earth, but his sustenance depends on Allāh ﷻ"** (Hood:6) Considering that I am also one of the creatures whose sustenance depends upon Allāh ﷻ, I occupied myself with paying what I owe to Allāh ﷻ and ceased to worry about what Allāh ﷻ has taken the responsibility to provide.

8. I have observed that all people have faith upon and put their trust in things which themselves have been created by Allāh ﷻ. Some have faith in their estates or business concerns, others in their own skill or craftsmanship, and there are still others who trust their own physical power and energy. I have read in the Holy Qur'ān that Allāh ﷻ says: **"And whosoever puts his trust in Allāh, He will suffice him."** (At-Talāq:3)

Shaqeeque Balkhi ﷺ thereupon said, "Hātim, may Allāh ﷻ bless you with divine aid for the performance of good deeds! I have viewed the teachings of Tawrāh, Injeel, Zaboor and the Holy Qur'ān, and I believe that these eight moral lessons form all that is really good and beneficial for man. Therefore, anyone acting upon these precepts will be deemed to have practised the learning contained in all four Scriptures revealed by Allāh ﷻ."

Sultān Salāh-ud-Deen Ayyūbi

The Power of Du'ās

Sultān Salāh-ud-Deen Ayyūbi was the leader of the Muslim army that was engaged in a heavy battle against the enemies. When Sultān Salāh-ud-Deen heard that the enemies were approaching his army with their huge army as well as their entire naval fleet, he became very worried. His army, the Muslims, was very small in number and did not have great resources like the enemies.

And so one night, Sultān Salāh-ud-Deen Ayyūbi went into Masjid Aqsā and spent the entire night in prayers and Du'ās. He begged for Allāh's help in overpowering the enemy. The next morning, as he was leaving Masjid Aqsā after praying Fajr Salāh, he saw a pious man nearby. Sultān Salāh-ud-Deen Ayyūbi walked up to the man and said, "Shaykh, a fleet of ships belonging to the enemies is about to attack our army and we do not have anything with which to defend ourselves. Will you please pray that we manage to defeat our enemy?"

"Salāh-ud-Deen, do not worry. The tears that you have shed last night have washed away the enemy's ships." And the next day the good news reached Sultān Salāh-ud-Deen Ayyūbi's ears. Yes, the pious man was indeed correct. The enemy's fleet of ship had sunk in a storm.

117

Justice is Achieved

The third Caliph of the Abbāsi rule, Al-Mahdi, was looking for a pious, knowledgeable Islāmic jurist, whom he could appoint for the position of Chief Judge in the city of Kufa. He was told about a man who possessed all of the said qualifications, a man who feared none but Allāh ﷻ. His name was Shareek Ibn Abdullāh ﷺ. The Caliph summoned him and then said to him when he came, "I indeed want to appoint you for the position of Chief Judge in Kufa." Shareek ﷺ said, "I certainly do not want to become a judge ever." Deeming it his right to pursue the matter further, Al-Mahdi asked, "Why?" Shareek ﷺ answered, "I fear that I will make a mistake in one of my judgements, for I am, after all, a mere man; and I fear that, as a result of that mistake, Allāh ﷻ will admit me into the Hellfire. I also fear that, if I issue a ruling against a leader or governor, my ruling will not be executed."

Caliph Al-Mahdi said, "You know that, if you strive to judge by the truth but you then make a mistake, Allāh ﷻ will not hold you accountable for it; rather, He will only hold you accountable if you judge unjustly on purpose, or if you judge, again on purpose, by other than what Allāh ﷻ has revealed. As for the execution and application of your rulings, I promise you that all of your judgements will indeed be executed, even if one of them is against me. If individuals such as you, righteous Islamic jurists do not agree to become judges, then who will take upon themselves such responsibilities? Would you like the ignorant ones, unjust ones or deviant ones to become judges? The sin of that happening will be upon

118

you, based on the fact that you will have, in that case, fled from applying the truth."

These arguments were too strong for Shareek ﷺ to ignore, and so he decided to accept the appointment of becoming Chief Judge of Kufa. The governor of Kufa at that time was Mūsā Ibn Eesā, the uncle of the Caliph Al-Mahdi. Every morning, Shareek ﷺ would go to the courthouse and judge between the litigants that came before him. True to the hopes of the Caliph, Shareek ﷺ was a very competent and just judge, and in regards to his rulings, he feared none but Allāh ﷻ.

Shareek ﷺ remained untroubled until he had to deal with a special case, the details of which are as follows. Situated on the shores of the Euphrates River in Kufa was a beautiful   garden. It was owned by a resident of Kufa; one day the governor of Kufa, Mūsā Ibn Eesā, decided that it would be nice to own that garden, especially since it was located right beside his castle. He made an offer for the property, but the owner refused to sell it. When the owner died, the garden then became the joint property of his children a number of sons and one daughter. Having failed to secure the purchase of the property from its previous owner, Mūsā Ibn Eesā went to the new owners and gave a generous offer to buy the garden. All of the sons of the previous owner were willing to sell the garden, but the daughter refused, despite the fact that Mūsā Ibn Eesā offered a huge sum of money, an amount that was much more than what the property was actually worth. And in spite of the daughter's refusal, the sons sold their shares to the governor. To protect her share of the garden, the young woman built a fence around it. Not satisfied at all by having part of the garden and not all of it, Mūsā Ibn Eesā decided to take the young woman's share of the property by force. He gave some instructions to his guards, who then proceeded to destroy the fence that the young woman had built.

The young woman then went to the courthouse and presented her case before Shareek ♯, who ordered that the governor should present himself in his courtroom, so that he could hear what both the plaintiff and the defendant had to say. As governor of Kufa, Mūsā Ibn Eesā felt insulted by the request, for why should he dispute a case with a mere common woman. Mūsā Ibn Eesā sent his chief guard to go in his place, ordering him to convey the following message to the judge: "How can you accept the claim of a woman when she has no witnesses with her?" Shareek ♯ looked angrily at the governor's representative, especially after hearing the message he came with. Shareek ♯ said, "Why are you here, when this matter has nothing to do with you? I requested the governor to come and not you; therefore your punishment is temporary imprisonment." The judge gave instructions to his guards, who then proceeded to arrest the governor's representative and to put him into prison.

When the governor found out what had happened, he sent some of Kufa's leaders to the judge, in order to try to reason with him and appease his anger. After they introduced themselves to him in his courthouse, they said, "The governor must not be treated like a common man; rather, he must receive special treatment, treatment that is in line with his position and status." Shareek ♯ replied,

"Before the law, all people are equal. As for you, you have inter-
fered with the law, and the punishment for that is temporary imprisonment." Again, Shareek 🕮 gave instructions to his guards,
who then arrested the men and put them into prison.

When Mūsā Ibn Eesā found out what had happened, he had finally
had enough, and so he set out with some of his men; they went together to the prison and released all those who were imprisoned
by the judge for interfering with the case. The prison guards, who
really couldn't do anything to stop the governor, went to Shareek
🕮 to tell him what had just occurred. He exclaimed, "I did not seek
out to be a judge; instead, it was the Caliph who coerced me into
taking the job, which I only accepted based on the condition that
all of my rulings will be executed." He gathered his papers, books
and his personal possessions, and then climbed his mount in
order to head towards the capital city, Baghdad.

When the governor found out that the judge was leaving, he became very afraid. For he knew that if the Caliph were to find out
what had happened, he would fire him from his post as governor,
regardless of the fact that he was the Caliph's uncle. And that is
why he rode out to catch up with the judge before he got too far;
he caught up with him on the outskirts of Kufa, and when he
reached him, he pleaded with him to return to Kufa, and he prom-
ised to fulfil all of his requests. Shareek 🕮 said, "I will not return
until all of the prisoners return to prison and until you present
yourself in my courtroom, in order to plea your case against the
woman who owns the garden."

Having no other realistic option in the matter, the governor accepted all of the judge's terms: the prisoners returned to prison,
and the governor presented himself at the courthouse. When both
the plaintiff and defendant were finished presenting their cases,
Shareek 卿 ruled in favour of the woman, ordering the governor to
rebuild her fence and to abstain from any future attempt at forcing
her to sell her share of the property. The governor accepted his ruling and quickly complied with its terms. When all was said and
done, Shareek 卿 ordered for the prisoners to be released from jail.
Later on, in what perhaps seemed to be an awkward meeting for
the governor, Shareek 卿 went to him and extended greetings of
peace to him. Shareek 卿 then said, "Do you now order me to do
anything?" Seeing the surprised expression on the governor's face,
Shareek 卿 said, "What happened before had to do with a right in
the Shari'ah, and my coming to you now has to do with the rights
of good manners."

Noor-ud-Deen 卿
The Ruler Standing before a Judge

Noor-ud-Deen Mahmood 卿 was a just and brave leader. He called
people to Islām and exhorted them to attend Islamic courts.

He used to say, "Before the Shari'ah, there is no difference between
a man of status and the common man."

He became known for this statement to the extent that the
businessman and men of high standing in society stopped going to

courts because they knew that they were now on an equal footing with others.

One day, as Noor-ud-Deen ﷺ was out practising the arts of war, he saw a man talking to another and pointing to him (i.e. to Noor-ud-Deen ﷺ). He sent a guard to ask what was the matter, he found out that the man was a messenger from the judge, who had come to inform Noor-ud-Deen that someone had a complaint against him and wanted to take the matter up before the judge, saying, "Deal with me as you would with any other person who comes to you for a ruling."

When he reached the judge, he stood side by side with the plaintiff, in the same manner that any other defendant would stand. We would be hard pressed in our times to imagine a ruler doing the same.

Imām Wāqidi ﷺ
Selflessness & Sympathy

Imām Wāqidi ﷺ was a great scholar of his time. Once he was in great financial difficulties, he was on the verge of poverty. Eid was fast approaching and there was nothing in his home. The elders could perhaps bear it patiently, but what about the children at home?

He says that he was compelled to ask for a loan from a trader friend of his. When his friend saw him, he understood the intention of the visit and placed 1,200 Dirhams in a bag and gave it to

Imām Wāqidi ﷺ.

When he reached home, a Hāshimi friend of his came by, who was also in a state of poverty and need. Wāqidi ﷺ said to his wife, "Distribute the contents of the bag into two equal parts and in this way both our needs will be sufficed."

His wife said, "This is strange! You have been to a normal layman who gave you 1,200 Dirhams and you are only giving him half of what a layman has given you! Do give him the entire bag."

Without any hesitation, Imām Wāqidi ﷺ gave the entire sealed bag, without even opening it to his Hāshimi friend. He took the bag.
Meanwhile, the trader friend of Imām Wāqidi ﷺ stopped by this Hāshimi, and said, "Eid is very close by, and there is nothing in the home. I would like a loan." The Hāshimi, offered him the very same bag, sealed.

When he saw his own bag, which was still sealed, he was astonished and sought to investigate the circumstances surrounding it.

He left the bag with the Hāshimi and came to Imām Wāqidi ﷺ, who narrated the entire episode to him. In reality, the trader also had nothing besides the bag and its contents, and he gave the entire bag to Imām Wāqidi ﷺ and sought a loan for himself, which is why he went to the Hāshimi. When the Hāshimi offered him the bag, the entire secret was revealed.

When this wonderful incident of selflessness and sympathy reached the Wazeer of the country, Yaḥyā Ibn Khālid, he took 10,000 Dinārs and said, "Two thousand is for Wāqidi, two thousand for the Hāshimi, two thousand for the trader and the balance four thousand for Wāqidi's wife, who was the most worthy and deserving of it."

"And they prefer others over themselves, even though poverty be their lot." (59:9)

These were those people who appreciated the value of Islāmic character, such that when a non- Muslim saw their behaviour he accepted Islām willingly.

Ideal Ameer

A pious person once asked Abū Ishāq Ibrāheem ﷺ, "Shaykh! I wish to travel with you." Abū Ishāq Ibrāheem ﷺ accepted the man's request and said, "However, one of us will have to be the Ameer (leader) so that everything runs smoothly."

"Then you must be the Ameer," the man said. To this, Abū Ishāq Ibrāheem ﷺ said to the man, "Then you must obey me."

The pious man relates the story further. He says, Whenever we reached a stop, Abū Ishāq Ibrāheem ﷺ would tell me to sit down and then fetch water himself. Because it was winter, he would gather firewood himself, light a fire and do all the other work. He never gave me permission to help him, because the condition was that he would give the instructions and I should obey them.

When heavy rain fell on the journey, he took off his shawl and held it over me all through the night so that I would not get wet. Although I was very embarrassed about this, I could do nothing because of our agreement.

The following morning, I told him that I was now the Ameer. "That's fine," he replied. However, when we reached the next stop, he again took all the work upon himself. "Why are you disobeying the Ameer?" I asked. He replied, "Disobedience is when one tells the Ameer to serve himself."

He then behaved like this throughout the long journey to Makkah. When we eventually reached, I was so embarrassed by the wonderful manner in which he treated me that I ran away from him. However, he saw me in Minā and said, "Son! One should show love for a friend just as I had done for you."

Shams-ud-Deen Altamish ﷺ
Allāh ﷻ Granted me Four Qualities

When Qutb-ud-Deen Bakhtiyār Kāki ﷺ passed away, there was great sadness and grief amongst the people. The body was prepared for burial and taken to a large field. There was a sea of people and they could be seen as far as the eye could see.

When the time arrived for the Janāzah Salāh to be performed, a man stepped forward and announced, "I am the person who has to carry out the will of Qutb-ud-Deen Bakhtiyār Kāki 👑 and I wish to read to you what he wanted." All the people present fell silent.

"He has stated that only that person should lead his Janāzah Salāh who has the following qualities in him:

1.   He must never have missed the first Takbeer for any Salāh in his lifetime (i.e. he always started every Salāh with the Imām).
2.   He must never have missed a single Tahajjud Salāh.
3.   He must never have looked at a non-Mahram woman (a woman who he is not allowed to look at) with an evil glance.

4.   He must never have missed the four Rak'at Sunnah Salāh before Asr."

There was a long silence before someone stepped forward and went up to the body of Qutb-ud-Deen Bakhtiyār Kāki 👑. "O Qutb-ud-Deen Bakhtiyār Kāki! Although you have passed away, you have embarrassed me in front of all these people today. It is before all these people that I take an oath in Allāh's 🕌 name that I have all four of these qualities. This is only by the grace of Allāh 🕌."

When the people looked at the man, they saw that it was the king Shams-ud-Deen Altamish 👑.

127

If a king is able to lead such a life of piety, what stops shopkeepers and office workers like us from doing the same? May Allāh ﷻ give us all the ability to do good. Āmeen!

A Very Special Dream

History books contain the mention of an amazing incident that took place in the year 557. At the time, 'Abbāsi dynasty was experiencing a sharp decline. As the lands of the Muslims became plagued by weaknesses and even chaos, some Christians got together and plotted to remove the Prophet's ﷺ body from his grave and to transport it back to their own lands, in what would obviously be a serious blow to the morale of the Muslims. For this diabolical plot, they sent two men to Madeenah, both of whom disguised themselves in Moroccan garments and claimed to be travellers who came to visit the holy city.

The two men stayed in a well-known house that was adjacent to the Holy Prophet's ﷺ Masjid. In order to blend in with the surroundings, they performed acts of worship in a noticeable manner, always hoping to be seen by others in order to gain their trust. But on the inside, they were plotting to achieve the task for which they had been sent.

Having come up with a plan that, at least in their minds, was sure to work, they began to execute it. They secretly began to dig a tunnel from inside their house, and by continuing to dig, they hoped to eventually reach the Holy Prophet's ﷺ grave. Every day, they would dig a little bit, placing the extra dirt in bags. They of course did not want to be seen by anyone when they would dispose of the extra dirt, and so they would get rid of it while they would take their daily walk in Al-Baqi', the famous graveyard of Madeenah. As they would walk through the graveyard, they would slowly pour out the dirt from underneath their cloaks. And all the while they would be giving others the impression that they were visiting the graveyard in order to remember death and the Hereafter. At times, they would also spill the excess dirt into a well that was near their home. After many days of secret toil, the two men were finally near the grave of the Holy Prophet ﷺ. Feeling sure now that they would succeed in their mission, they began to concentrate their thoughts on concocting a plan to actually transport the Holy Prophet's ﷺ body to their homeland. But they could plot and plan as much as they wanted, for Allāh ﷻ had other plans for them, and what He wills, He does.

Far away from Madeenah, the ruler during that era, Noorud-Deen Muhammad Ibn Zanki ﷺ saw a troubling dream. In that dream, he saw the Holy Prophet ﷺ pointing to two men of red complexion, and instructing Noorud-Deen Muhammad ﷺ to protect him from them. Noorud-Deen Muhammad ﷺ then woke up, both frightened and agitated. In order to calm his nerves, he stood up to pray, after which he went back to sleep. But during that night, he saw the same dream three times. When he woke up the third time, he summoned for one of his ministers to come to him. That minister was Jamāl Uddeen Al-Moosili ﷺ, a wise minister who was a prac-tising, righteous Muslim. When the ruler finished telling him about his dream, Jamāl Uddeen ﷺ said, "This is concerning something that is happening in Madeenah. Go now to the Holy Prophet's ﷺ city and keep secret what you have seen."

For the remainder of that night, Noorud-Deen Muhammad ﷺ made preparations to leave. 20 mounts were loaded and 20 men, one of them being Jamal Uddeen ﷺ, made preparations to go with their leader. They made the journey from Syria to Madeenah in 16 days. When they reached their destination, Noorud-Deen Muhammad ﷺ went to Masjid Nabawi and prayed, but as of yet, he had no idea what he should do about his dream.

His minister, Jamal Uddeen ﷺ, asked him if he remembered what the two people he saw in his dream looked like. Noor-ud-Deen Muhammad ﷺ said that he remembered them clearly, and that if he were to see them now, he would certainly recognize them. Jamal Uddeen had a plan to apprehend the two men, and he immediately put it into action. When the inhabitants of Madeenah were gathered in the Masjid, Jamal Uddeen ﷺ made the following announcement: "Indeed, the ruler has brought with him a great deal of wealth that has been earmarked for charity. Have the poor ones among you register their names, and then bring them, so that each can take his fair share." While each person came to take a share of the handout, Noorud-Deen Muhammad ﷺ was standing right there, looking at each person, in the hope of seeing one or both of the men he saw in his dream. Many people came and went, but Noorud-Deen Muhammad ﷺ saw no one who resembled either of the two men.

He then asked, "Is there anyone left who still has not taken his share?" Someone said, "There remains two men from Morocco; they refuse to take their share, and indeed, they are both very righteous." "Bring them to me!" were the immediate words that came out of

Noorud-Deen Muhammad's 🕮 mouth. When the two men were brought before him, Noorud-Deen Muhammad 🕮 immediately recognized them: they were the two men that the Holy Prophet 🕮 pointed to in his dream. Noorud-Deen 🕮 asked them, "Where are you from?" They said, "We are from the West, and we have come here in order to perform Hajj. After we arrived, we decided to stay here this year.

Perhaps their plot was not exactly clear to Noorud-Deen 🕮 at that moment, but he knew they were guilty of something, and so he continued to interrogate them, hoping that they would confess their crime, whatever it was. But they kept to their story, and with no proof against them, Noorud-Deen 🕮 couldn't justly take any steps against them. Noorud-Deen 🕮 then ordered for their home to be searched. After a thorough search, they found nothing peculiar save a large amount of money that the two men had stored in their home. As everyone began to file out of the two men's home, Allāh 🕮 guided Noorud-Deen 🕮 to look at the wooden floor. One of its boards was loose, and Noorud-Deen 🕮 stooped down to have a closer look. He realised that the board was not attached solidly to the floor, and so he picked it up. The people of Madeenah were shocked to see the entrance of a tunnel and even more shocked to see where it led to, for they had been certain that the two men were righteous Muslims.

After being beaten by the furious ruler, the two men confessed that they weren't really from the West, but were instead two Christians who had been sent by their leaders with a great deal of wealth that was paid to them upfront for the job of removing the Holy Prophet

131

ﷺ from his grave and transporting the body back to their lands. Noorud-Deen ﷺ ordered for the two men to be executed and for the tunnel to be blocked up and filled with dirt. When these two orders were executed, he returned to Syria. And Allāh ﷻ knows best.

Shaykh Qādhi
Thanā-ullāh Pānipati ﷺ
(D.1225 AH/1810 CE)

The great Shaykh, the Imām, the Allāmah, the Muhaddith Thanā-ullāh Uthmāni Pānipati ﷺ was one of the most erudite scholars (of undivided India). He was from the progeny of Shaykh Jalāl-ud-Deen Uthmāni ﷺ, through whom his family tree reaches the blessed Companion Sayyidunā Uthmān Ibn Affān ﷺ. He was born, and grew up, in the town of Pānipat where he memorised the Holy Qur'ān and studied Arabic for a while with the teachers of the town. He then travelled to the city of Delhi and studied under the legendary master and Imām Shāh Waliullāh Ibn Abdur-Raheem Umari Dehlawi ﷺ, better known as 'Shāh Waliullāh', from whom he acquired the science of Hadeeth.

He read Fātihah al-Farāgh and completed his formal education in the sciences of the Deen at the young age of eighteen years. Thereafter he adopted the company of Shaykh Muhammad Ābid Sunnāmi ﷺ, from whom he received training in Tareeqah. Through the training imparted by the latter Shaykh, Qādhi Thanā-ullāh Pānipati ﷺ reached the level known in Tareeqah as the 'annihilation of the heart' (Fanā al-Qalb). He then turned to the great Shaykh Mirzā Mazhar Jān-e-Jānān Alawi Dehlawi ☙, who trained him to the final stage in the Mujaddidiyyah Tareeqah. Shaykh Jān-e-Jānān ☙ had tremendous affection toward, and love for, Qādhi Thanā-ullāh Pānipati ☙ and gave him the title of Alam al-Hudā (the flag of guidance).

He said regarding Qādhi Thanā-ullāh Pānipati ☙, "Awe from his piety and Taqwa has engulfed my heart. He is one who implements and propagates the Shari'ah, illuminates Tareeqah and possesses angelic traits. Even the angels revere him." He once said, "If Allāh ☙ was to seek from me a gift, I would present Thanā-ullāh to Him." In recognition of his oceanic knowledge of Fiqh and Hadeeth the Imām and Muhaddith Shaykh Abdul-Aziz Ibn Waliullāh Dehlawi ☙ gave him the title of 'Bayhaqi of the age'.

Shaykh Ghulām Ali Alawi Dehlawi ☙ says in his book al-Maqāmāt, "Qādhi Thanā-ullāh Pānipati ☙ was second to none amongst his contemporaries in Taqwa and piety. He used to exert himself in his devotions to Allāh ☙, praying a hundred Rak'at and reciting a seventh portion of the Holy Qur'ān every day. All this he used to do alongside other forms of Dhikr, Murāqabah (meditation) and his preoccupation with teaching, lecturing, writing and adjudication." He says elsewhere in the same book, "With his sharp and clear intellect, fine wisdom and extraordinary personality he had reached the stage of Ijtihād in Fiqh and Usool. He had authored a detailed book in Fiqh, in which he elaborated each Mas'alah with its source and substantiating evidences whilst pointing out the opinions of the four Imāms in Fiqh in that particular Mas'alah. He had also authored a smaller book entitled al-Akhdhu bil-Aqwā in which he recorded all the stronger opinions of the schools of Fiqh. He had also authored an exegesis (Tafseer) of the Holy Qur'ān in seven large volumes."

Shaykh Muhsin Ibn Yahyā Turhuti 🌸 says in al-Yāni al-Jāni, "Qādhi Thanā-ullāh Pānipati 🌸 was a jurist, a jurisprudent, one who had renounced the world and a Mujtahid. He had his own opinions in the (Hanafi) school of law. He authored magnificent works in Fiqh, Tafseer and Zuhd. His Shaykh was proud of him."

His famous works include: At-Tafseer al-Mazhari in seven volumes, a two-volume detailed book in Hadeeth, Māla-Budda-Minhu in Hanafi Fiqh, Irshād Uth-Tālibeen in Tasawwuf, Tadhkirah al-Mawtā wal-Quboor, Tadhkirah al-Ma'ād, Haqeeqat al-Islām, a treatise on the ruling on singing and music, a treatise on the unlawfulness of the practice of Mutah, a treatise on Ushr and Khirāj and a few other treatises. He passed away during Rajab 1225 AH (1810 CE) in his home town of Pānipat. May Allāh 🌸 grant him and all the masters mentioned in this article the highest of Paradise.

Shaykh Ashraf Ali Thānwi 🌸

Shaykh Ashraf Ali Thānwi 🌸 was born on the 5th of Rabeeuth-Thāni 1280 A.H. (1863) in the village of Thāna Bhawan. He lost his mother at a tender age and was brought up by his father in a fairly wealthy background. His father took great pains in teaching him and his younger brother discipline and good character.

From a young age he had a great desire for Salāh. Even whilst playing, he used to imitate the worshippers, e.g. he gathered all his friends shoes, placed them in a line, put one shoe in front of the line and expressed his happiness that the shoes were performing Salāh. He also had a great inclination to deliver lectures. On his way to the shops, he used to enter any Masjid, ascend the Mimbar and deliver a Khutbah (sermon).

At the age of 12, he began performing Tahajjud and other Nafl Salāh and Wazeefah. His love for Deen was sown by his initial teacher, Shaykh Fātih Muhammad Sāhib 鐚. After learning the basic Kitābs from his uncle and Shaykh Fātih Muhammad 鐚, he proceeded to Deoband to complete his studies and qualified at the tender age of 20 years. From his student days he became famous for his intelligence and sharp-wittedness. He never wasted his time in futile play and amusement. Such was his burning desire to obtain knowledge that he learnt certain Kitābs, which he could not study during class times, from his teachers while they were performing Wudhu. Shaykh Ashraf Ali's 鐚 teachers were all great luminaries of their time. The most important amongst them was Shaykh Muhammad Ya'qoob Sāhib 鐚 from whom he achieved the greatest amount of knowledge and spiritual benefit. He learnt Qirat (recitation) from the well-known Qāri Muhammad Abdullāh Sāhib Muhājir Makki 鐚 and mastered it to such an extent that it became difficult for the listener to distinguish between the recitation of the student and the teacher.

After qualifying, he spent 14 years in Kanpur teaching, writing and propagating to the people. During this period, thousands of students quenched their thirst at this 'ocean of knowledge'. Although Shaykh Ashraf Ali Thānwi ﷺ was still very young, the people of Kanpur respected and honoured him tremendously and it was at that time that he became famous. His discourses were greatly appreciated and were being printed in the form of booklets. Very few scholars in the history of Islām have had so many of their discourses printed.

During his student days in Deoband, he desired to make a pledge at the hands of Shaykh Rasheed Ahmad Gangohi ﷺ who refused, saying that it would harm his studies. Shaykh Ashraf Ali ﷺ then wrote a letter to Hāji Imdādullāh ﷺ in Makkah urging him to make Shaykh Gangohi ﷺ accept the pledge. Hāji Imdādullāh ﷺ by means of a letter instead accepted Shaykh Ashraf Ali ﷺ as his disciple.

When Shaykh Ashraf Ali ﷺ accompanied his father for Hajj one year after qualifying, he renewed his pledge at the hands of Hāji Imdādullāh ﷺ. After his return from Makkah, he continued teaching and propagating while his desire for Dhikr intensified.

He used to deliver lectures while standing for five to six hours and sometimes even seven hours continuously.

In 1315 A.H. he left Kanpur and on the advice of his spiritual mentor, Hāji Imdādullāh ﷺ, returned to Thāna Bhawan. This was all part of the divine plan of the Creator so that the Khanqah of Hāji Imdādullāh ﷫ would once again be re-inhabited. This was the termination of the first phase of his life which was devoted more to religious education.

The second phase which began with his return to Thāna Bhawan was devoted more to imparting spiritual benefits to the masses. Shaykh Ashraf Ali ﷫ wrote books in every field whether it be Tafseer or Tasawwuf, Fiqh or Tajweed. All his works total more than a thousand. In the field of Hadeeth, he did not write any voluminous work directly because he had many assistants. In this way the voluminous 'I'lā-us-Sunan' was written under his guidance. Regarding this Kitāb, he said that if this Madrasah does not do other work besides the writing of this book, it will be a great achievement because it is a unique work.

Perhaps very few Muslim homes do not possess 'Behishti Zewar' and 'Munājāte-Maqbool', two of Shaykh's famous books. His Tafseer 'Bayānul Qur'ān' is unparalleled. Shaykh Anwar Shāh Kashmeeri ﷫, well known for his in-depth knowledge, used to say that after reading Bayānul Qur'ān, he developed a desire to read Urdu books.

Sincerity

Although Shaykh Ashraf Ali ﷫ wrote such a large number of books, he did not earn a penny from them. All his work was solely for the pleasure of Allāh ﷻ. He granted full permission to anyone who desired to print his books. Some of his works have been through hundreds of editions. Shaykh ﷫ used to say that all praises are due to Allāh 🏵 because all the essential work has been done. The path towards Deen has been cleared for centuries. Inshā-Allāh, his books, discourses and advice will be of assistance in religious matters for future generations. This is all due to the blessings of Hāji Imdādullāh 🏵.

Inspiration

On 20 Jumādal Oolā 1346 A.H. whilst performing Fajr Salāh, he was inspired about the effects of certain acts. If the Muslims practised these acts, their calamities could be overcome. Shaykh 🏵 subsequently gathered 25 principles and had them printed in a booklet called 'Hayātul Muslimeen'.

Although Shaykh 🏵 wrote over 1000 books, he had this to say, "I never thought of my books being a means of salvation for me. However, with regards to Hayātul Muslimeen, I have a strong feeling it will be a means of my salvation. I regard it as the earning and capital of my entire life."

Death

Shaykh 🏵 spent his entire life serving Deen in every field. It is for this reason that he has been conferred the titles of Hakeemul Ummat and Mujaddidul-Millat. After blessing the earth for 83 years with his presence, he passed away on 16 Rajab 1362 A.H. (20 July 1943). The Janāzah Salāh was performed by Shaykh Zafar Ahmad Uthmāni 🏵.

Shaykh Ashraf Ali Thānwi 🏵
Advice for the Students of Deen

"Some of our Students of Deen labour under the idea: 'We shall make Amal (practise the laws) after completion of studies.' This idea is totally erroneous. The sin which you are unable to abandon today, the obedience which you refuse to adopt today and your lack of control of the Nafs today because you leave it free will increase further later. Later (i.e. after studies) to a greater extent will you be unable to abandon the sin. You will then not be able to adopt obedience nor control the Nafs.

On the contrary, it is simpler to act today (while you are engaged in the pursuit of Knowledge). As time passes, Akhlāq Razeelah (evil habits) will become stronger and rooted.

All the complaints and criticism which the general public has, against the Scholars are on account of their corrupt moral condition. By Amal (practise of Deen) I am not referring to abundance of Nawāfil, Salāh, Sawm, etc. By the Grace of Allāh 🏵, you do engage in these acts of worship. The focus of my attention does not concern these acts. The focus of my attention is Akhlāq (Moral character).

Abandon all sins of the heart and gaze, etc. Be concerned with measures to remedy these illnesses of the heart. Never come near to greed. As a result of this disease of greed you fall greatly in the eyes of the people. Wherever there is the slight sign of this state

(i.e. of being despised by wealthy people) do not venture near them.
Never adopt any measures to gain their favour even if you are in dire need (financial adversity). Be completely independent."

Shaykhul-Islām Sayyid Husain Ahmad Madani ﷺ
(1296-1377 AH/1879-1957 CE)

Born in Bāngar, Mao, the Indian district of Annow on 19 Shawwāl 1296 AH (5 October 1879 CE), Shaykh Sayyid Husain Ahmad Madani ﷺ began his primary Islamic education in Faizabād. At the age of twelve, he travelled to the Dārul-Uloom at Deoband where he studied the intermediate and higher level books of the traditional Dars-e-Nizāmi course. During his seven and a half years at the Dārul-Uloom, Shaykh Sayyid Husain Ahmad Madani ﷺ studied about sixty books, twenty four of which were taught by the legendary Imām of undivided India, Shaykhul-Hind Mahmūdul-Hasan ﷺ (1268-1339 AH/1851-1920 CE).

He describes in his two volume Urdu autobiography (Naqsh-e-Hayāt: A Sketch of My Life) how, as a young student at the Dārul-Uloom, he was very close to Shaykhul-Hind and had free access to the latter's home. Similar affection was shown by all his illustrious teachers at the Dārul-Uloom.

As a young Ālim (scholar), Shaykh Sayyid Husain Ahmad Madani ﷺ offered his allegiance of Tasawwuf (Bay'ah) at the blessed hands of the Imām of his age, dubbed 'the Abū Haneefah of the era', Shaykhul-Mashāikh Rasheed Ahmad Gangohi ﷺ (1244-1323 AH/1829-1905 CE).

In 1316 AH (1898 CE) he travelled with his parents and siblings to the radiant city of Madeenah Munawwarah, where his father, Sayyid Habeebullāh ﷺ settled permanently in fulfillment of his yearning to undertake Hijrah. On their way to Madeenah Munaw-warah, the family spent some days in the blessed company of the master of all the Indian Mashāikh of his age, Hāji Imdādullāh Muhājir Makki ﷺ (1233-1317 AH/1817-1899 CE) in the Holy city of Makkah Mukarramah.

In 1318 AH (1900 CE) Shaykh Sayyid Husain Ahmad Madani ﷺ and his eldest brother, Shaykh Sayyid Muhammad Siddiq ﷺ (1288-1331 AH/1871-1913 CE), were summoned to India by Shaykh Rasheed Ahmad Gangohi ﷺ. Shortly after arrival, Imām Rasheed Ahmad Gangohi ﷺ wrapped Amāmahs (turbans) around their heads and granted them formal Khilāfah (or Ijāzah) in Tasawwuf. They both remained in India for two years before returning to Madeenah with a group of Hājis.

When Shaykh Sayyid Husain Ahmad Madani ﷺ and his family embarked on their very long journey to Madeenah, his beloved teacher, Shaykh Mahmūdul-Hasan, walked with them to the train station. He advised Shaykh Sayyid Husain Ahmad Madani ﷺ

never to give up teaching the Islamic sciences, wherever he may be and whatever the circumstances. He held fast to this advice. Once settled in Madeenah, despite the severe tribulations that he and his family underwent, Shaykhul-Islām began teaching some books of the Islamic sciences in the Masjid of the beloved Prophet ﷺ.

In the sections of his autobiography detailing his academic pursuits in Madeenah, he describes his surprise at the relatively poor academic abilities of those who were lecturing in the Holy Masjid at the time, compared with what he had been accustomed to in India.

No sooner had he commenced his lectures on the various Islamic sciences that his fame spread far and wide. Students began to desert the other lecturers and flocked to his lectures. They would marvel at the depth and richness of his oceanic knowledge of all the Islamic sciences and his grounding in the Fiqh of all four schools of sacred law. Consequently, he found himself the target of much envy and malice.

Students, many of them from Madeenah, Turkish, Bukhāri, Qāzāni, Kazākhi, Egyptian and Afghāni origins - would find themselves mesmerised by his lectures on a wide spectrum of texts, many of which he himself had not studied previously, including in Ilmun-Nahw (grammar); the Ājrūmiyyah, Hallān, Kafrāwi, Alfiyyah, Sharh Ibn Aqeel, Sharh Alfiyyah Ibn Hishām. In Ilmul-Ma'āni wa'l-Bayān (the science of Arabic eloquence); Sharh Uqoodul-Jumān, Risālah Istiārāt, Risālah Wad'iyyah li'l-Qādhi. In

Ilmul-Badi (another branch of Arabic eloquence); Badiyyat Ibn Hajar.

In Hanafi Fiqh; Nūrul-Idhāh, Multaqa'l-Abhur, Durar etc. In the jurisprudence of the Shāfi'ee and Māliki schools; Sharh Jam'ul-Jawāmi-li'l-Subki, Sharh Mustafā-ul-Usool, Waraqāt, Sharh Muntahā'l-Usool. In Aqāid (Islamic creed); Mūsāmarah Sharh Mūsāyarah, Sharh Tawāli'ul-Anwār, Jawharah. In Mustalah-ul-Hadeeth (principles and technicalities of Hadeeth) Alfiyyah Usool-ul-Hadeeth, Bayqūniyyah and many other texts in the sciences of Farā'id; (law of inheritance), Mantiq (logic), Tafseer (exegesis of the Holy Qur'ān), Hadeeth (Prophetic traditions) and Kalām (theology).

Due to the ever increasing insistence of students, he would deliver fourteen lectures a day; five in the morning, three or four after Zuhr prayers, two after Asr prayers, two after Maghrib prayers and one after Ishā prayers. He would only sleep for three to three and a half hours, sometimes suspending all lectures and sleeping for six to seven hours, thereby refreshing himself for a full week. All this he did without any form of salary, upon the guidance of his spiritual mentor, Shaykh Rasheed Ahmad Gangohi ﷺ.

Circumstances of the Muslims (of India) compelled Shaykh Sayyid Husain Ahmad Madani ﷺ to return to India. There, under the leadership of his illustrious teacher, Shaykh Mahmūdul-Hasan ﷺ, he dedicated himself to the nationwide movement for freedom of India. In 1335 AH (1917 CE) he and Shaykhul-Hind ﷺ were arrested in Hijāz (in modern day Saudi Arabia) and imprisoned in Malta. After his release in 1338 AH (1920 CE), he became even more dedicated to the fight for India's freedom.

When Shaykhul-Hind 🌸 passed away that same year, Shaykh Sayyid Husain Ahmad Madani 🌸 continued his illustrious teacher's struggle for India's independence and in 1360 AH (1941 CE) was appointed president of the Jamiatul-Ulamā of India, a role in which he served until his demise in 1377 AH (1957 CE).

Upon the final instruction of his beloved teacher Shaykhul-Hind 🌸, Shaykh Sayyid Husain Ahmad Madani 🌸 taught Hadeeth at a Madrasah in Calcutta for a short period before moving to Sylhet (in modern day Bangladesh), where, during the six years that he lived there, he taught Hadeeth, served as the prime and unparalleled spiritual mentor of the Muslims of the region and carried on his mission to see an independent India.

In 1346 AH (1927 CE), he accepted the post of grand Shaykh of Dārul-Uloom Deoband as Shaykhul-Hadeeth. An estimated 3,856 students studied Hadeeth under him. Many thousands of Muslims pledged the allegiance of Tasawwuf (Bay'ah) at his hands, from whom a total of 166 were granted formal Khilāfah (or Ijāzah) in Tasawwuf by Shaykhul-Islām.

After the independence of India, Shaykh Sayyid Husain Ahmad Madani 🌸 distanced himself from politics and devoted all his time and energy on the teaching of Hadeeth, spiritually reforming the

Muslims and Da'wah. In recognition of his sacrifices for India, in 1373 AH (1954 CE) the government wished to confer Shaykh Maulānā Sayyid Husain Ahmad Madani ﷺ an honorary official title. He declined, saying that the acceptance of such an award was contrary to the way of his pious predecessors (the Salaf and Akābir).

His sacrifices and selflessness for the people of India generally, and for the Muslims of India specifically, remain till this day unparalleled. His legacy remains alive today throughout the breadth and width of not just south Asia, but the world.

This legendary master passed away in 1377 AH (1957 CE) at his home in Deoband. His funeral prayer was led by the great Shaykhul-Hadeeth Muhammad Zakariyyā Kāndhalwi ﷺ (1315-1402 AH/1898-1982 CE). He was laid to rest beside his teacher Shaykhul-Hind Mahmūdul-Hasan ﷺ and Imām Hujjatul-Islām Muhammad Qāsim Nānotwī ﷺ (1248-1297 AH/1833-1880 CE), the founder of the Dārul-Uloom, within its precincts in Deoband.

Shaykh Anwar Shāh Kashmiri ﷺ

Lineage
Shaykh Anwar Shāh Kashmiri ﷺ was from the progeny of Shaykh Mas'ood Narwari ﷺ whose ancestors were from Baghdad. They migrated to Multān and Lahore and eventually settled in Kashmir. Shaykh Kasmiri's ﷺ father, Shaykh Muhammad Muazzam Shāh ﷺ was a renowned scholar and a famous saint of Kashmir.
Education

145

After studying Persian and basic Islamic knowledge at home, he proceeded to Hazarah in the N.W. Frontier Province to complete his Arabic studies. However, his thirst for knowledge was not quenched there either and this made him travel in 1307 A.H. to the "Mother of all Institutes" namely, Darul Uloom Deoband. He studied there for four years and derived maximum benefit from all the luminaries of his time. The following are some of the great legends from whom he attained the knowledge of Islām: Shaykhul-Hind Mahmoodul-Hasan 🌸, Shaykh Ishāq Amritsari 🌸 and Shaykh Ghulām Hazarwi 🌸.

In Kashmir
On his return from Hajj, he established Madrasah Faize-Ām in Kashmir. He lived there for three years during which thousands of people benefited from his company. He was invited to the annual gathering of Darul Uloom Deoband after which he was appointed a teacher. He taught the Hadeeth book 'Abū Dāwood' and 'Saheeh Muslim' for several years without any salary. When Shaykhul-Hind 🌸 left for Makkah, Shaykh Kashmiri 🌸 was appointed his deputy. He now had the responsibility of teaching Saheeh Al-Bukhāri and Tirmizi.

Qualities
Shaykh Kashmiri 🌸 became well-known for his intellect, phenomenal memory and depth of knowledge. Shaykh Shabbir Ahmad Uthmāni 🌸 once said in an assembly in Dhabel, "If any Egyptian or Syrian has to ask me if I have seen Hāfiz Ibn Hajar, Shaykh Taqiud-Deen or Shaykh Izzud-Deen Ibn Abdis-Salām, I will reply

in the affirmative because I have seen Shaykh Anwar Shāh 鐕 - only the era is different. Had Shaykh Kashmiri 鐕 been alive in the sixth or seventh century, his virtues and feats would have glorified the pages of history. I feel as if Hāfiz Ibn-Hajar, Shaykh Taqiud-Deen and Shaykh Izzud-Deen 鐕 have passed away today."

Shaykh Husain Ahmad Madani 鐕 said, "I have met Scholars from India, Hijaz, Iraq, Egypt and Syria and had discussions with them on various Masā'il, but I have not found anyone who can match the encyclopaedic depth of knowledge of Shāh Sāhib (Shaykh Anwar Shāh)."

The famous Egyptian Scholar, Shaykh Sayyid Rashid Rada 鐕 once said in Deoband, "By Allāh 鐕, I have never seen a person like him."

Shaykh Sayyid Atāullāh Shāh Bukhāri 鐕 used to say, "The Caravan of the Sahābah 鐕 was travelling and left Shāh Kashmiri 鐕 behind."

Shaykh Sayyid Sulaimān Nadwi 鐕 said, "Shāh Sāhib 鐕 was like an ocean whose surface is calm while the inside is full of gems."

Commenting on his phenomenal memory, Shaykh Manāzir Ahsan Gilāni 鐕 said that Shāh Sāhib 鐕 had committed approximately 40,000 Arabic verses to memory. Shaykh Idrees Kandhelwi 鐕 remarked that Shāh Sāhib's memory was so remarkable that whatever he read or heard once was forever preserved in his memory as if he was the Imām Zuhri 鐕 of his time. When Imām Zuhri 鐕 used to walk the streets of Madeenah, he used to put his fingers in his ears. When asked the reason for this, he said that whatever entered his ears did not leave. "I close my ears so as not to hear the noise of the marketplace."

The famous poet of the East, 'Allāmah Iqbal commented that 500 years of Islāmic history have been unable to produce the likes of Shāh Sāhib ﷺ. Shaykh Habibur Rahmān Uthmāni ﷺ used to call him a 'mobile library'. His reading speed was so astonishing that he used to read 200 pages of Musnad Ahmad daily and quote its Ahādeeth in his lessons without referring to it again. He read the entire Fathul-Qadeer (8 Volumes) in 20 days together with answering objections raised against the author. Thereafter for the rest of his life, he did not refer to it although he quoted it extensively in his lessons.

Shaykh Zāhid Kawthari ﷺ, after studying some of Shāh Sāhib's works, commented thus, "After Shaykh Al-Munāwi (author of Faidul-Qadeer), there has not been such a Muhaddith (as Shaykh Kashmiri) in the Ummah who can derive delicate Masā'il from the Ahādeeth."

He was an embodiment of the Sunnah and practised it meticulously. The words 'Hasbun-Allāh' (Allāh ﷻ is sufficient) and 'Allāh-Azzawajall' were constantly on his lips.

Students
Probably his most unparalleled virtue is that he produced peerless Scholars and Muhaddithoon. During his 18 years stay at Deoband, no less than 2000 students quenched their thirst at this 'well' of

knowledge. A complete list of all his students will require a book for enumeration. Some of his famous students were:

Shāh Abdul Qādir Raipuri, Mufti Shafee, Maulānā Manāzir Ahsan Gilāni, Maulānā Idrees Kandhelwi, Maulānā Badre-Ālam, Maulānā Hifzur-Rahmān, Maulānā Yūsuf Binnori, Mufti Ateequr-Rahmān, Maulānā Manzoor Nu'māni, Mufti Muhammad Hasan, Maulānā Habibur-Rahmān and Qari Tayyib Sāhib 🌸.

Besides serving Deen in the field of education and Tableegh, Shaykh Kashmiri 🌸 has also written some outstanding works, the most memorable of which is probably his commentary of Saheeh Bukhāri viz Faidul-Bari. One of his most outstanding student, Shaykh Yūsuf Binnori 🌸 has written an excellent book in Arabic, Nafhatul Ambar on his life.

Of his progeny, the more well known are Maulānā Anzar Shāh and Maulānā Azhar Shāh, both of whom were teachers of Hadeeth at Deoband. He remained in Deoband until 1345 A.H. after which he left for Dhabel with some scholars and a large group of students due to some differences with the management . He taught Hadeeth in Dhabel till 1351 A.H. On 2 Safar 1352, he left this temporary abode at the approximate age of 60.

In the Company of
Shaykh Mufti Tālib Uddin 🕮
(1361-1431 AH/1942-2010 CE)

Shaykh Mufti Tālib Uddin Ahmad 🕮 was amongst the many pious scholars of Islām who became successful through seeking knowledge and propagating it. He was born in the year 1942 in the village of Shataihal, Dinarpur, Nabigonj in the county of Habigonj, Bangladesh. His father Qāri Alā-Uddin Ahmad was a prominent Qāri of his community, well respected by the elders, famously known as 'Boro Miah Sāhib'. His mother was the Rābiya Basri of her time, very well known for Ibādah, good morals and character.

Shaykh Mufti Tālib-Uddin Ahmad 🕮 received his primary Deeni education at home from his respected father. He went further on to study in the famous Islamic institutes known as Jāmiah Qāsimul-Uloom Bohubal and Jāmiah Arabiyah Dinarpur Balidara, Habigonj.

To quench his thirst of knowledge, he travelled to Pakistan in 1962 and studied in the institute Darul-Uloom Tendwala established by Khateeb Pakistan Shaykh Ihtishāmul Haq Thānwi 🕮. There he studied under great luminaries, the likes of Shaykh Zafar Ahmad Uthmāni, Shaykh Idrees Kandhalwi, Shaykh Jamsheid and Shaykh Abdur-Rahmān Kamilpuri 🕮.

In the year 1964, he studied Mishkāt Shareef in Jāmiah Fathiyya Lahore. He gained the privilege of learning from great scholars like Shaykh Habibur-Rahmān Lahori and Shaykh Ghulam Mahmood.

150

In 1965, he studied his final year of Hadeeth under the world renowned Hāfizul-Hadeeth Allāma Abdullāh Darkāsti ؆ in Markazul Uloom Wal-Fuyooz in Raheem Yār Khān. His other great teachers include Shaykhul-Hadeeth Shaykh Ibrāheem ؆ and Shaykh Mufti Ghulām Haydar ؆.

In the year 1966, he did the Iftā course under the supervision of Shaykh Mufti Rasheed Ahmad Ludhyānwi ؆ in Ashraful-Uloom Nāzim-Ābād North Karachi. During his Iftā course, he benefitted from the company and knowledge of the Grand Mufti, Mufti Shafee Sāhib ؆. He used to go and attest and verify Fatāwa and Masā'il from him. Occasionally he would also attend the Majlis of Shaykh Mufti Mahmood Sāhib ؆, Mufti Abdullāh ؆ and Shaykh Ghulām Gaus Hazārvi ؆.

After his graduation as a qualified scholar and Mufti, he was immediately chosen by his seniors to commence teaching at the institute where he originally once studied, Qāsimul-Uloom Bohubal. There, he was promoted to the post of senior teacher. In the following year, he moved to Al-Arabiyah Husainiyah Dhaka Dakhin. He was assigned to teach the senior Kitābs of Fiqh and Hadeeth in that institute.

After six years of Deeni Khidmat (service) he was invited to take the role of principal in the institute Al-Arabiyah Husainiyah Boytakhal.
After a decade of Deeni Khidmat as a principal in the institute, he migrated to Saudi Arabia. A group of people from England went

to perform Hajj and they realised the potential and expertise of Mufti Sāhib and thus invited him to migrate to England so they could benefit from his knowledge and company. Hence, he moved to England as an Imām after staying 14 months in Saudi Arabia. He became the main Imām in Jāmi Masjid, Middleton, Oldham.

In the Masjid he commenced the Dars (discourses) of Tafseer, Hadeeth and Fiqh and soon became recognised for his sharp knowledge and inspirational talks. He was invited across the country for lectures and resolving intricate issues of marriage, divorce, inheritance, domestic violence etc.

In 1994 Shaykh Mufti Tālib Uddin ﷺ was appointed the principal of Dārul-Qur'ān Madrasah, Baniyachong, Habigonj, Bangladesh. With the grace of Allāh ﷻ and Mufti Sāhib's persistence and hard work, the Jāmiah became a well renowned and credited Madrasah for knowledge and Tarbiyah (upbringing) where many chose it as a first choice for study. During his time as principal, the Jāmiah progressed rapidly and underwent numerous construction and expansion work providing more space and facilities for the students. At present there are 710 students studying in the departments of Hifz and Theology classes.

In 1997, Mufti Sāhib founded and established the famous Markazi Masjid, Al-Khazrā in Oldham. This soon became the centre point for the work of Dawah, spirituality and knowledge. Many leading Islamic scholars have paid a visit to this place to witness the hard work of Mufti Sāhib.

Izhār Haq is an organisation which was founded by Mufti Sāhib and is currently run from the Masjid. Izhār Haq as understood by its name was established to proclaim the truth and eradicate evil and Bid'ah (innovation) from the Deen. It was the tireless effort and sacrifice of Mufti Sāhib which progressed and promoted the work of Izhār Haq throughout the UK.

Mufti Sāhib in order to complete his thirst of knowledge and spirituality, took Bay'ah (oath of allegiance) to one of the leading disciples of Shaykhul-Islām Shaykh Husain Ahmad Madani ﷺ, Shaykh Abdul Mannan Ghunoy. He progressed through the path of spirituality very rapidly and was awarded by his Shaykh with the mantle of Khilāfah and Ijāzah in the year 1978.

Mufti Sāhib for quite a number of years had been ill and bed ridden, even then he continued to impart the knowledge and wisdom which Allāh ﷻ bestowed upon him.

It was Saturday evening the 3rd of July 2010 when the health of Mufti Sāhib seriously deteriorated. Family members were called to the hospital and in their presence, he read out a few couplets expressing his long desire to meet his Creator and then breathed his last. Innā lillāhi wa-innā ilayhi-rāji'oon.

The news of his demise spread like wildfire across the UK and abroad. I immediately with many of my colleagues arrived at the hospital and within minutes the hospital became overcrowded with relatives, friends and scholars.

The funeral prayer took place on the following day after Zuhr Salāh in the Millennium Centre Oldham. Mufti Junayed Ahmad Sāhib, the eldest son of Mufti Sāhib lead the funeral prayer. Thousands of people from across the UK attended the funeral prayer. May Allāh 卿 have mercy on Shaykh Mufti Tālib-Uddin, elevate his status in Jannah, and bless his family and everyone associated with him.

Mufti Sāhib was well known to everyone and was classed as one of the senior Muftis of the UK. Intricate and complicated issues used to be referred to him and he always came out with a solution. I was very fortunate to be acquainted with Mufti Sāhib due to being his son-in-law. I have witnessed many great qualities and attributes in the life of Mufti Sāhib, the most prominent being his generosity and kindness. Volumes could be written about his lofty character and attributes and I hope that a detailed biography will be available in the near future.

He has left behind 4 sons out of whom 3 are qualified scholars and 7 daughters, out of whom 4 are qualified Ālimahs. All his six son-in-laws are scholars who are engaged in the work of Deen. They will all Inshā-Allāh be Sadaqah Jāriyah for him including the institute Dārul-Qur'ān, Al-Khazrā Markazi Masjid and the thousands of students and disciples who have benefited from this ocean of knowledge.

I pray to Allāh 卿 that He gives us the ability and strength to follow in the footsteps of Shaykh Mufti Tālib Uddin 卿 and our pious predecessors. Āmeen!

In the Company of
Shaykh Husain Ahmad Umarpuri ﷺ
(1364-1431 AH/1945-2010 CE)

Shaykh Husain Ahmad ﷺ, famously known as Shaykh Umarpuri ﷺ left us all orphans and went to meet his Lord the Most High, on the morning of Thursday 26th of August 2010 (corresponding to 16th of Ramadhān 1431 AH). This great scholar and pious friend of Allāh ﷻ departed from us at the very blessed time of Tahajjud.

Subhān-Allāh! What a blessed death, in the state of a Mūsāfir (traveller), in the blessed month of Ramadhān and at the time of Tahajjud!

Ever since my childhood I have been fortunate to meet and accompany pious saints and scholars, and Shaykh Umarpuri ﷺ was one of the distinguished ones.

I first got to know him through his son-in-law Shaykh Abdul Hameed from Luton, UK, who was a very close friend of mine from our student days in Dārul-Uloom Bury, UK. He was fortunate to marry one of Shaykh Umarpuri's ﷺ daughters after his graduation. I very well remember the lengthy letter Shaykh Abdul Hameed sent from Bangladesh in which he stated what a renowned scholar Shaykh Umarpuri ﷺ was.

I was privileged to accompany Shaykh on many occasions and lis-

155

ten to his talks. Subhān-Allāh! his talks and lectures were so mes-
merising and immensely influential.

The most remarkable moments for me were, when I sat in his
company with other scholars, the knowledge and wisdom he
possessed and commanded, it virtually left everyone spellbound
for hours on end.

In the year 2007, when I visited Bangladesh, I was honoured to
meet him in Kiampur, Sylhet, at his niece's marriage, which was
with my beloved student Mujibur-Rahmān. After I had solemnised
the Nikāh, Shaykh Umarpuri 卐 concluded the ceremony with an
emotional supplication.

Thereafter, Shaykh Umarpuri 卐 insisted that I accompany him to
his village, but due to my busy schedule, I was unable to comply.
Nevertheless, I was fortunate to meet him subsequently for the following 3 years. On every occasion when he visited Bradford, UK,
he would deliver a speech at our local Masjid – Tawak'kulia Jāmi
Masjid and then I would accompany him wherever he would
travel around Bradford.

Before Ramadhān in 2010, I invited Shaykh Umarpuri 卐 to our
institute Jāmiah Khātamun Nabiyeen in Bradford UK. He
delivered an inspirational and spiritual discourse on Saheeh Al-
Bukhāri.

Everyone present at the discourse were amazed by Shaykh

Umarpuri's ﷺ high level of knowledge and wisdom. He left us all astonished by the explanation of ILM. He began by asking, "What is the meaning of ILM?" He continued, "The Harkat (Kasra) on the letter AIN stands for the effort and sacrifice we need to give initially to acquire knowledge. The (Sukoon) on the letter LĀM stands for steadfastness, meaning whilst in the process of acquiring knowledge we need to be focused towards our studies without diverting our attention to anything else.

The two Harkat (Dhamma) on the letter MEEM means, once we acquire knowledge, we must double our effort and sacrifice to convey the knowledge we have attained." - Subhān-Allāh!

After the discourse, I requested Shaykh Umarpuri ﷺ to join us to perform I'tikāf at our local Masjid for the following Ramadhān, which he readily and happily accepted. I was overjoyed and began to inform all the scholars and students about this golden opportunity.

It was decided that after his return from London, he would stay in Bradford for the last days of Ramadhān, and during the I'tikāf he would conduct lessons of Bukhāri for the scholars and students. But according to the decree of Allāh ﷻ, it wasn't meant to be and Allāh ﷻ had planned better things for Shaykh Umarpuri ﷺ.

Shaykh Umarpuri ﷺ said in his last and which was to be his final speech, "People today don't value and appreciate the Sylheti Ulamā (scholars). After Shaykh Noor-ud-Deen Gohorpuri ﷺ who is left in Sylhet? Only me and Shaykh Kiampuri are left. One day we will go too." Who knew Shaykh Umarpuri 鐊 was going to depart this world after saying these words? Indeed, to Allāh 鐊 we belong and to Him we shall return.

It was after the Tarāweeh Salāh where he was addressing a gathering in the famous Ford Square Masjid in London, when he suddenly felt an acute pain in his head, due to which he was rushed to the hospital. From then on Shaykh Umarpuri 鐊 went into a state of coma for a week and passed away on Thursday 26th of August 2010.

The news of his departure spread like wildfire across the UK and abroad, to which we became completely dumbfounded.

The funeral prayer took place on Friday 27th August 2010 (17 Ramadhān 1431) after the Jumu'ah Salāh at the Ford Square Masjid. Myself and many other Ulamā from across the UK and abroad notably Shaykh Mukhlisur-Rahmān Kiampuri from Bangladesh (Shaykh Umarpuri's 鐊 brother-in-law), attended the funeral prayer. An estimate of around 10,000 people attended the funeral prayer. May Allāh 鐊 have mercy on Shaykh Umarpuri 鐊, elevate his status in Jannah, and bless his family and everyone associated with him.

In my view, I have witnessed that the most prominent and remarkable quality in the life of Shaykh Umarpuri 鐊 was his noble and lofty character.
Although I was much inferior to many of his students, he was very

loving and affectionate towards me and always respected and honoured me more than I deserved. This was the case for every scholar; he held them in very high esteem.

When he spoke about his teacher Shaykh Noor-ud-Deen Gohorpuri ﷺ and other pious predecessors, he would mention many anecdotes and incidents regarding their lives which would leave the audience ecstatic.

Allāh ﷺ bestowed Shaykh Umarpuri ﷺ with great intellect and wisdom. For a period of over 40 years he taught Bukhāri, Muslim, Tirmizi, Ibn Mājah and many other classical Islamic books to thousands of students, producing scholars who went on to engage in the service of Deen across the globe. He has left behind these scholars as well as eight sons and seven daughters as Sadaqah-Jāriyah on his behalf.

I pray to Allāh ﷺ that He gives us the ability and strength to follow in the footsteps of Shaykh Umarpuri ﷺ and our pious predecessors, Āmeen!

Shaykh Sarfarāz Khān Safdar ﷺ
"From the Cradle to the Grave"
Unquenchable Thirst for Knowledge

Writing whilst the funeral arrangements were being made, Shaykh Zāhid Ar-Rāshidi writes about the inspirational academic aspect of his illustrious father's personality:

"My revered father Shaykh Muhammad Sarfarāz Khān Safdar ﷺ had been bedridden for the last eight or nine years. Despite this, by the grace of Allāh ﷺ his memory did not fail him and his academic interests remained the same till the end. His eyesight had deteriorated severely and he had trouble in recognising people, but if a person was introduced, he would recall everything regarding that person. He would then ask that person even the most minor things. I would generally have the opportunity to visit him for a brief while on Friday evenings. Whenever he felt better, he would ask for a book to be read to him. I would read any book of Hadeeth to him. I would always fear reading to him, as the slightest of errors would not pass unnoticed or unchecked. A few months prior to his demise he asked, "Would you happen to have a reliable (Arabic) dictionary?" I asked, "What will you do with a dictionary in this condition?" He replied, "Sometimes the need for a dictionary arises." I purchased a dictionary and presented it to him and he was very pleased with it. On another occasion he asked, "Will *Al-lu'lu wa'l-Marjān* be available in the bookshops?" I replied in the affirmative. I then purchased it for him.

Last month when I was setting off for my trip to the United Kingdom, I informed him that I intended to perform Umrah on the way back. He was pleased at hearing this, prayed for me and said, "I have heard that *Musnad Abī Ya'lā* has now been published. If you are able to, could you get me a copy of it?"

I searched for it in several bookshops in Makkah Mukarramah and Madeenah Munawwarah, but could not find it. On my way back I said to my host in Jeddah, Qāri Muhammad Aslam Shehzād, my wife's brother-in-law, "I do not feel like returning home without the book." We both then visited the bookshops in Jeddah together. After visiting two or three bookshops, we managed to find it. I was overjoyed by this find, but Qāri Sāhib was happier than me. He prevented me from paying for it and asked that I present it to my revered father as a gift from him.

I returned home on Thursday and as per my weekly routine I visited my father on Friday. He was feeling very unwell. When I showed him the book, he gestured that I place it where he had asked me to.

Only a few days ago, as per our routine, my brothers and I were by his bedside on Friday. He was feeling somewhat better. He asked me where such and such a verse was in the Holy Qur'ān. I told him where it was. I thought he would be enquiring about an issue related to that verse, but when he asked me a second question regarding it, I realised he was testing me. My younger brother Qāri Azīzur-Rahmān, who resides in Jeddah, was also there. I pushed him in front of me and hid myself. He then underwent a test. He was asked about several verses and the verses preceding them. We were extremely happy seeing our father so well and in such a good mood.

During my visits, he would usually ask about the state of the nation. In recent days, he had been very concerned about the state of Swāt (in the Afghan-Pak frontier province). He stayed abreast of

161

newspapers, and he would often ask questions relating to news items. He would read my regular newspaper columns and would comment on some of their contents. I once wrote in one of my columns that the Holy Prophet ﷺ is an 'ideal' for his Ummah. The next time I visited him, he asked me what the word 'ideal' meant. I replied that this was an approximate translation of the Arabic term *Uswatun-Hasanah*.

Once, while reading a Hadeeth to him, I got stuck on a word. I was surprised myself that this had happened when I had in fact previously read and taught the Hadeeth several times. When this happened, he told me what the word was and also explained the Hadeeth to me. Many a time, I have struggled to recall the precise wording of a Hadeeth and could not locate it in the books, but when I asked him he would tell me in which chapter of which book to look. I would then find it in that precise location. This is not from the days when he was well and healthy, but rather during the days when he was so ill that he could not turn on his side in bed himself. In such a condition, his memory remained so sharp that we would be left amazed by it.

Despite his immaculate and unparalleled proficiency in all the sciences of Islām, and despite having spent more than half a century teaching and serving Islām and the Muslims, Shaykh Muhammad Sarfarāz khān Safdar ﷺ would often express his sorrow at not having been able to teach to his heart's content. Shaykh Muhammad Aslam Shaykhūpūri writes of how when he visited Shaykh Safdar ﷺ a year prior to his demise, he asked whether he had any unfulfilled wishes. Shaykh Safdar ﷺ replied that there were many such wishes. Upon Shaykh's request to mention one such wish, Shaykh Safdar ﷺ stated that he had not had the opportunity to teach the primary level (small) books of the *Dars-e-Nizāmī* course. This was the unfulfilled wish and desire of a man who had spent half a century lecturing on the major books of Hadeeth, including the Sunan of Imām Abū Eesā At-Tirmizi ﷺ and the Jāmi' of Imām Muhammad Ibn Ismā'eel Al-Bukhāri ﷺ, and the text and Tafseer of the Holy Qur'ān to the Ulamā tens of times. He was, without an iota of doubt, an embodiment of the Hadeeth of the Holy Prophet ﷺ narrated by Sayyidunā Abū Sa'eed Al-Khudri ﷺ and reported in Tirmizi, in which the Holy Prophet ﷺ said, "A believer will never be content with (any amount of) good that he hears until he reaches his goal and final destination of Paradise." This unquenchable thirst for knowledge and desire to serve Islām and the Muslims in such a selfless manner is only the lot of the true Ulamā of the Ākhirah, the men of Allāh ﷻ, described by the Holy Prophet ﷺ as the 'heirs of the Prophets', when he said, "Indeed the Ulamā are the heirs of the Prophets, and indeed the Prophets do not leave behind a legacy of Dinārs and Dirhams, but they leave behind a legacy of knowledge. He who acquires it has indeed acquired a complete portion."

After describing the condition of Shaykh Safdar's ﷺ thirst for knowledge, Shaykh Aslam Shaykhūpūrī relates an incident that occurred only a few weeks prior to his demise. He says, "Shaykh Mufti Muhammad Rafī Uthmāni had come to visit Shaykh Safdar ﷺ. After greeting him, the first thing Shaykh Safdar ﷺ asked him

163

was, "The Shaykhul-Hadeeth of Jāmi'ah Ashrafiyyah (Lahore), Sūfi Muhammad Sarwar Sāhib has related such and such a Hadeeth from your revered father (Shaykh Mufti Muhammad Shafī 🌸). I am looking for its reference. Could you please identify its source?"

The condition of Shaykh Safdar 🌸 during his final days, described by his son Shaykhul-Hadeeth Aslam Shaykhūpūri, is reminiscent of the condition of the pious Ulamā of the early centuries such as Imām Abū Yūsuf Ya'qūb Al-Ansārī 🌸, the senior student of Imām Abū Haneefah Nu'mān Al-Kūfi 🌸, and that of Imām Ibn Mālik 🌸, the grammarian (Nahwi) on their death beds.

A student of Imām Abū Yūsuf 🌸, Al-Qādi Ibrāheem says, "Imām Abū Yūsuf 🌸 was ill. I went to visit him and found him unconscious. When he regained consciousness, he asked me, "O Ibrāheem, what do you say regarding a certain issue in Fiqh?" I said, "Even in such a condition?!" He replied, "That is not a problem at all. Let us discuss a matter of knowledge, perhaps someone will be relieved by it." He then asked, "O Ibrāheem, what is better when pelting the pillars (of Jamarāt) in Hajj, to pelt on foot or mounted on a beast?" I replied, "Mounted on a beast." He said, "Incorrect." I then said, "On foot." He again replied, "Incorrect." I said, "Please tell me. May Allāh 🌸 be pleased with you." He said, "The pillar, after the pelting of which, one should stop and supplicate (say a Du'ā) - it is best to pelt it on foot. As for the pillar, after the pelting of which, one should not supplicate- it is best to pelt it mounted on a beast." I then took leave from him. I had not even reached the door of his house when I heard the sound of people crying over him. He had died. May Allāh ﷻ have mercy upon him."

It is said regarding Imām Ibn Mālik ؓ, the grammarian (Nahwi), author of the *Alfiyyah* in the science of Nahw, that he committed to memory several verses of poetry on the day he died. Some have specified that they were eight verses, communicated to him by his son.

The Last Email
of the Late Āsif Khalifah
An eye-opener for our youth of today!

Āsif Khalifah was a young person from Bradford who passed away at the age of 23 in October 2010. A family member retrieved one of his last emails that he had sent to his friend just before his death. One of his friends emailed him seeking advice on how his day can go smoothly. This email is worth pondering over as it contains much useful advice and serves as a lesson for all of us. The email is as follows:

"My Friend! I have got a remedy for you, if you want a good day and you want good things to happen to you then this is what you should do. This is how my days go by:

1) Before retiring for bed (at night) I think of Fajr Salāh, I make

Niyyat (intention) that I am going to read it because you will be rewarded for making the intention.

2) I Recite 11 times (takes 40 seconds):

لَا اِلهَ اِلَّا اَنْتَ سُبْحٰنَكَ اِنِّى كُنْتُ مِنَ الظَّالِمِيْنَ

(Lā-ilāha illa anta subhānaka innee kuntu minazzālimeen)

Trans: There is no God but You, Glory be to You, surely I am amongst the wrong doers.

3) Thereafter I recite once (takes 5 seconds):

اَللّٰهُمَّ لَكَ الْحَمْدُ كَمَا يَنْبَغِىْ لِجَلَالِ وَجْهِكَ وَلَعَظِيْمِ سُلْطَانِكَ

(Allāhumma lakal hamdu kamā yambaghee li-jalāli wajhika wa-liazeemi sultānika)

Trans: O Allāh! For You is (all) praise as Your Majestic Countenance and Your Great Kingdom is worthy of it.

4) Then I recite once (takes 8 seconds):

اَللّٰهُمَّ اِنِّى اَسْأَلُكَ بِاسْمِكَ الله وَ بِاسْمِكَ الرَّحْمٰنِ وَ بِاسْمِكَ الرَّحِيْمِ وَ بِاَسْمَاءِكَ الْحُسْنٰى كُلِّهَا مَا عَلِمْتُ مِنْهَا وَ مَا لَمْ اَعْلَمْ اَنْ تَغْفِرَلِى

(Allāhumma innee as'aluka bismikallāhi

166

wa-bismikar-Rahmāni wa-bismikar-Raheemi wa-bi-asmā-ikal husnā kullihā mā alimtu minhā wa-mā-lam a'lam an-taghfiralee)

Trans: O Allāh! I beseech You with Your name Allāh and with Your name Ar-Rahmān and with Your name Ar-Raheem and with all Your Beautiful names of what I know and of that which I do not know that You forgive me.

5) Then when I leave my house (to go to work) I recite the Masnoon Du'ā once (takes 3 seconds):

بِسْمِ اللهِ تَوَكَّلْتُ عَلَى اللهِ وَلاَحَوْلَ

وَلاَ قُوَّةَ اِلاَّ بِاللهِ

(Bismillāhi tawak'kaltu alallāhi wa-lāhawla wa-lā quwwata illā billāhi)

Trans: In the name of Allāh, I place my reliance in Allāh and there is no power nor might except with Allāh.

6) Thereafter, as I am walking towards the bus stop I begin to recite Sūrah Yāseen by heart and whilst I am stood at the bus stop, I have completed its recitation. It takes me around 7 minutes to recite but if you look into the Holy Qur'ān it will take you around 10-11 minutes.

7) Thereafter, I recite the four Quls and recite Sūrah Ikhlās thrice, as (mentioned in a Hadeeth) you will receive the reward of reciting

the entire Qur'ān once and thereafter Āyatul-Kursi.

8) Then I recite Tasbeeh on the bus or when I am walking which is: Subhān-Allāh 100 times, Alhamdulillāh 100 times and Allāhu-Akbar 100 times.

9) Then I recite Durood, but ensure that you recite a lot of Durood throughout the day as there are many blessings in it.

10) When I get to work and sit on my chair, I recite:

رَبِّ اشْرَحْ لِىْ صَدْرِىْ وَ يَسِّرْ لِىْ اَمْرِىْ وَاحْلُلْ عُقْدَة مِنْ لِّسَانِىْ يَفْقَهُوْا قَوْلِىْ

(Rabbishrah-lee sadree wa-yassirlee amree wahlul
uqdatam-millisānee yafqahū qawlee)

Trans: O my Lord! Open my chest for me (grant me confidence) and make my task easy for me and remove the impediment from my tongue so they understand my speech.

I also recite:

اَللّٰهُمَّ اَعِنِّى عَلىٰ ذِكْرِكَ وَ شُكْرِكَ

وَحُسْنِ عِبَادَتِكَ

(Allāhumma a'innee alā dhikrika wa-shukrika
wa-husni ibādatika)

168

Trans: O Allāh! Assist me upon remembering You (abundantly) and being grateful to You and upon worshipping You in the best manner.

It may sound a lot to read but trust me, it will not take no more that 15 minutes. Your day will pass smooth and quick without any problems and Allāh ﷻ will assist you in what you do throughout the day."

May Allāh ﷻ reward brother Āsif Khalifah for this wonderful advice, forgive all his sins, make it a means of salvation for him in the Hereafter and grant him Jannatul Firdaws. Āmeen!
May Allāh ﷻ also grant us the ability to follow his advice, Āmeen!

I sincerely request all the readers to remember him and his family in your Du'ās.

Other titles from JKN PUBLICATIONS

Your Questions Answered

An outstanding book written by Shaykh Mufti Saiful Islām. A very comprehensive yet simple Fatāwa book and a source of guidance that reaches out to a wider audience i.e. the English speaking Muslims. The reader will benefit from the various answers to questions based on the Laws of Islām relating to the beliefs of Islām, knowledge, Sunnah, pillars of Islām, marriage, divorce and contemporary issues.

Hadeeth for Beginners

A concise Hadeeth book with various Ahādeeth that relate to basic Ibādāh and moral etiquettes in Islām accessible to a wider readership. Each Hadeeth has been presented with the Arabic text, its translation and commentary to enlighten the reader, its meaning and application in day-to-day life.

UK RRP: £3.00

Du'ā for Beginners

This book contains basic Du'ās which every Muslim should recite on a daily basis. Highly recommended to young children and adults studying at Islamic schools and Madrasahs so that one may cherish the beautiful treasure of supplications of our beloved Prophet 鹵 in one's daily life, which will ultimately bring peace and happiness in both worlds, Inshā-Allāh.

UK RRP: £2.00

How well do you know Islām?

An exciting educational book which contains 300 multiple questions and answers to help you increase your knowledge on Islām! Ideal for the whole family, especially children and adult students to learn new knowledge in an enjoyable way and cherish the treasures of knowledge that you will acquire from this book. A very beneficial tool for educational syllabus.

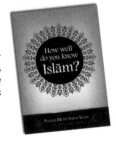

Treasures of the Holy Qur'ān

This book entitled "Treasures of the Holy Qur'ān" has been compiled to create a stronger bond between the Holy Qur'ān and the readers. It mentions the different virtues of Sūrahs and verses from the Holy Qur'ān with the hope that the readers will increase their zeal and enthusiasm to recite and inculcate the teachings of the Holy Qur'ān into their daily lives.

UK RRP: £3.00

Other titles from JKN PUBLICATIONS

Marriage - A Complete Solution

Islām regards marriage as a great act of worship. This book has been designed to provide the fundamental teachings and guidelines of all what relates to the marital life in a simplified English language. It encapsulates in a nutshell all the marriage laws mentioned in many of the main reference books in order to facilitate their understanding and implementation.

UK RRP: £5.00

Pearls of Luqmān

This book is a comprehensive commentary of Sūrah Luqmān, written beautifully by Shaykh Mufti Saiful Islām. It offers the reader with an enquiring mind, abundance of advice, guidance, counselling and wisdom.

The reader will be enlightened by many wonderful topics and anecdotes mentioned in this book, which will create a greater understanding of the Holy Qur'ān and its wisdom. The book highlights some of the wise sayings and words of advice Luqmān ﷺ gave to his son.

UK RRP: £3.00

Arabic Grammar Beginners

This book is a study of Arabic Grammar based on the subject of Nahw (Syntax) in a simplified English format. If a student studies this book thoroughly, he/she will develop a very good foundation in this field, Inshā-Allāh. Many books have been written on this subject in various languages such as Arabic, Persian and Urdu. However, in this day and age there is a growing demand for this subject to be available in English .

UK RRP: £3.00

A Gift to My Youngsters

This treasure filled book, is a collection of Islamic stories, morals and anecdotes from the life of our beloved Prophet ﷺ, his Companions ﷺ and the pious predecessors. The stories and anecdotes are based on moral and ethical values, which the reader will enjoy sharing with their peers, friends, families and loved ones.

"A Gift to My Youngsters" – is a wonderful gift presented to the readers personally, by the author himself, especially with the youngsters in mind. He has carefully selected stories and anecdotes containing beautiful morals, lessons and valuable knowledge and wisdom.

UK RRP: £5.00